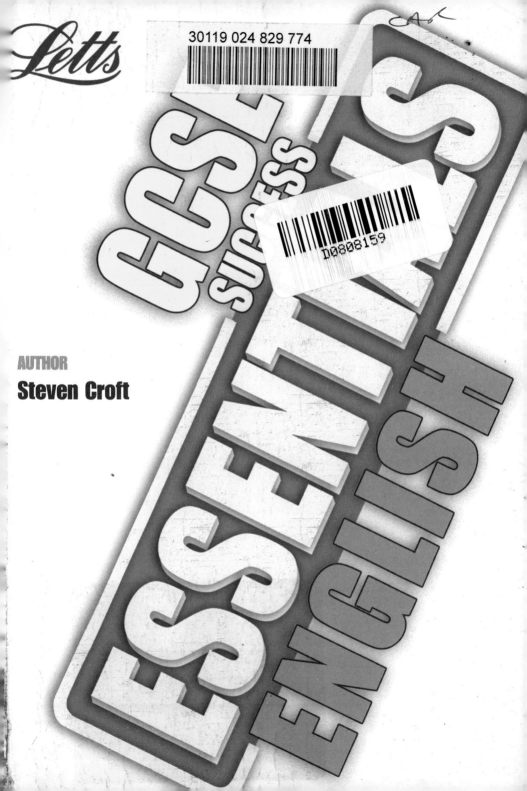

Letts

GCSE
success
ESSENTIAL
ENGLISH

AUTHOR
Steven Croft

Introduction

Contents

Quick Reference

Tricky Topics

Writing a story

Non-fiction

Poetry

Shakespeare

Fiction

Original writing

Speaking and Listening coursework

Glossary

Introduction

This book has been written as a GCSE revision product for students studying GCSE English and English Literature courses. It also supplements the *GCSE English and English Literature Success Guide* and *GCSE English and English Literature Questions and Answers Success Guide*. Included are some useful tips with an emphasis on those areas that students find most difficult. There is also information to enable students to do better in their English coursework.

The book has been split into several sections.

Essential information

The book is useful to keep at hand during English lessons, while doing your homework and while revising for the GCSE examination. The Quick Reference section contains essential information on English language that you will have to use throughout the course.

Tackling the tricky topics

Students sometimes find some areas of the course a little tricky and are not always entirely clear how to deal with them. We have called these areas Tricky Topics. This book highlights several Tricky Topics and helps you master them. Being able to handle these areas will help boost your confidence.

Get to grips with coursework

Since the coursework element of GCSE English counts for 40% of the total mark (20% Written coursework and 20% Speaking and Listening), it is important to take time over it and get as high a mark as possible. The sections on Preparing Your Coursework and Speaking and Listening will help you.

Learn your lingo

To succeed really well, you need to understand and use the correct terminology. The glossary at the end of this book will help you when you come across unfamiliar words to do with literary analysis, grammar and more. Use it in lessons or when doing your homework.

How to revise English

Concentrate on the topics you need to work on most. However, you should not miss any topics out as most of the specification will be examined in each set of exams.

Here are a few tips to help you plan your revision.

Planning

- Find out the dates of your English examinations.
- Make an exam and revision timetable.
- Look at a copy of the specification. You may be able to get a copy from your teacher. If not, specifications are available online and can be downloaded from the appropriate Examination Board site. Go through and make a list of topics. Look at the list and decide honestly which ones you are happy with and which need more work. Concentrate on the latter. Deal with them one at a time.
- For each topic, make some brief notes (no more than one side of A4) of key points as you revise. Keep these notes as they will be useful for last-minute revision.
- Try and write out these key points from memory. Check what you have written against your list. Have you missed anything out?

Revising

- Revise in short bursts of about 30 minutes, followed by a short break.
- Memorise any problematic spellings or quotations you need to learn.
- Learning with a friend is easier and more fun.
- Try sample questions of all types. Make sure you practise extended writing questions – these are the questions requiring long answers and candidates often have difficulty with them.

Taking the examination

- The night before the exam, try to have an early night. Examinations are tiring and require you to be alert.
- Get all of your equipment – pens, pencils, pre-release material or set texts if required – ready the day before.
- Arrive in good time.
- Follow all the instructions on the exam paper.
- If you have a choice of question in the exam, make sure that you look at and think about all the questions carefully before making your choice. A strong start will give you confidence.

We hope you find this book useful during your coursework, revision and as you prepare for the exams. *Good luck!*

Parts of speech and sentences

Parts of speech

All English words can be divided into different groups according to the functions they perform. These different groups of words are called **parts of speech**. There are ten parts of speech in the English language.

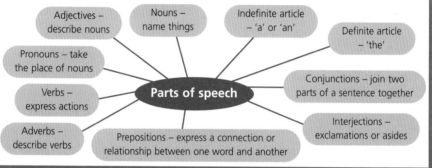

Adjectives – describe nouns

Nouns – name things

Indefinite article – 'a' or 'an'

Definite article – 'the'

Pronouns – take the place of nouns

Conjunctions – join two parts of a sentence together

Verbs – express actions

Parts of speech

Interjections – exclamations or asides

Adverbs – describe verbs

Prepositions – express a connection or relationship between one word and another

Identifying the parts of speech

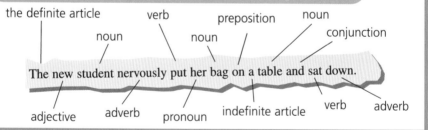

the definite article

verb

preposition

noun

noun

noun

conjunction

The new student nervously put her bag on a table and sat down.

adjective

adverb

pronoun

indefinite article

verb

adverb

Sentences

Sentences are the units that we use to express our ideas – particularly in writing.

There are three basic kinds of sentence:

1. **Commands** – e.g. Get out of here!
2. **Questions** – e.g. Are you going out tonight?
3. **Statements** – e.g. The train was very late.

For more help see GCSE Success Guide page **14**

Identifying the sentence structure

SIMPLE SENTENCES

A **simple sentence** has just one finite verb (a finite verb is a verb that has a subject).

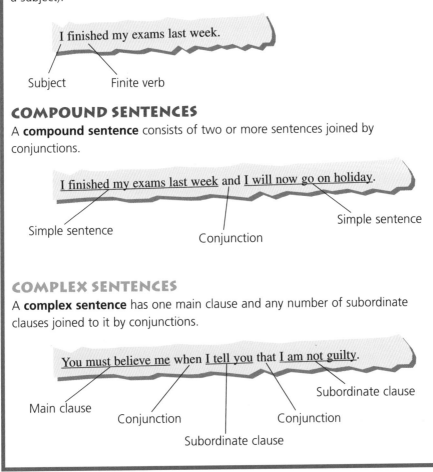

I finished my exams last week.

Subject   Finite verb

COMPOUND SENTENCES

A **compound sentence** consists of two or more sentences joined by conjunctions.

I finished my exams last week and I will now go on holiday.

Simple sentence   Simple sentence

Conjunction

COMPLEX SENTENCES

A **complex sentence** has one main clause and any number of subordinate clauses joined to it by conjunctions.

You must believe me when I tell you that I am not guilty.

Main clause   Subordinate clause

Conjunction   Conjunction

Subordinate clause

REMEMBER

A **phrase** is a group of words that does not contain a finite verb.

A **clause** is a group of words with a finite verb.

A **main clause** can make complete sense on its own.

A **subordinate clause** gives additional information.

For more help see GCSE Success Guide pages 14–15

Paragraphs

What are paragraphs?

If you are writing more than a few sentences you need to divide your work into **paragraphs**.

- Paragraphs make it clear to the reader when we start to write about a new thing, a new topic, or a new aspect of the thing being discussed.
- Paragraphs separate items, such as examples, from the main text.
- Paragraphs are used when quotations are introduced.

How long is a paragraph?

The length of a paragraph depends entirely on what you have to say – they can be long or short depending on the context and content. Single sentence paragraphs can be effective occasionally, but they should not be over-used in your work. The use of single sentence paragraphs throughout a piece of writing is not to be recommended. Equally, very long paragraphs can confuse the reader.

The benefits of paragraphs

- Using paragraphs makes you think about how you are going to structure your writing.
- This means that you need to plan out in advance what you are going to say and what each paragraph will cover.
- As you write you need to think carefully about how your ideas link together from paragraph to paragraph. This can help the fluency of your writing.
- Paragraphs help your reader to understand what you have written. It is easier to read and understand the content of each paragraph and to see how one idea leads on to the next. Un-paragraphed text is hard to read because it is presented as a solid block of writing.
- Paragraphs are also used to structure dialogue and make it clearer to read.

Features of a paragraph

1. Each paragraph is about a separate topic or separate aspect of a topic.

2. Each paragraph begins by giving an indication of what it is about or what is going on.

3. The paragraph then goes on to develop this idea in more detail.

4. One paragraph often links to another. However, if you move on to a completely different topic there will be more of a break.

5. Paragraphs normally consist of two or more sentences, although sometimes a single sentence paragraph can make the point effectively.

Useful words and phrases

Words that help put your ideas in order:
- firstly, then, so far, secondly, next, eventually, subsequently, at last, at length, afterwards

Words to make a contrast:
- but, nevertheless, alternatively, despite this, on the contrary, however, yet, the opposite, instead, whereas, on the other hand

Words to sum up:
- in brief, in summary, throughout, in all, on the whole, to sum up, overall, finally, to recap, to conclude, in the end

For more help see GCSE Success Guide pages 20–21

Nouns

Types of noun

Nouns are words that 'name' things such as people, places, objects and ideas. Nouns can be divided into several different types, each of which performs a particular function.

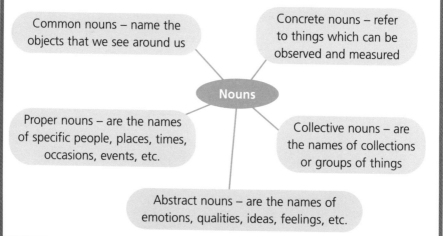

Common nouns – name the objects that we see around us

Concrete nouns – refer to things which can be observed and measured

Nouns

Proper nouns – are the names of specific people, places, times, occasions, events, etc.

Collective nouns – are the names of collections or groups of things

Abstract nouns – are the names of emotions, qualities, ideas, feelings, etc.

Common and proper nouns

Common and proper nouns differ in three main ways:

1. Proper nouns are written with an initial capital letter (although not all words with initial capital letters are proper nouns). The use of capitals can change the meaning in a major way:

'the Manchester road' → one of possibly several roads that lead to Manchester

'the Manchester Road' → the name of a specific road

2. Proper nouns do not usually have a plural form, e.g. 'Manchesters', but most common nouns do, e.g. 'books', 'chairs'.

3. Proper nouns are not usually used with determiners, e.g. 'a Manchester', 'the Italy', whereas common nouns are, e.g. 'the book', 'a city'.

Note: Sometimes proper nouns *can* behave like common nouns in special circumstances, e.g. 'I don't like Mondays', 'I know a James'.

Singular and plural

ADDING AN 'S'

Most nouns change from singular to plural by adding an 's'.

book(s)   telephone(s)   computer(s)   table(s)
idea(s)   video(s)   pen(s)   cup(s)   basket(s)

CHANGING THE VOWEL

Some nouns change their vowel in the plural.

woman → women

man → men

foot → feet

goose → geese

mouse → mice

tooth → teeth

louse → lice

ADDING 'EN'

Three nouns are made plural by adding 'en'.

child → children

brother → brethren

ox → oxen

> Keep a **spelling log book** for any plurals you find problematic. See page 30 for some other basic spelling rules and exceptions.

CHANGING 'F' TO 'V'

knife → knives

wife → wives

leaf → leaves

half → halves

ADDING 'ES'

fox → foxes

glass → glasses

SAME FORM FOR SINGULAR AND PLURAL

sheep

deer

aircraft

Pronouns

What are pronouns?

Pronouns are words which take the place of nouns where appropriate within a sentence. The use of pronouns within a sentence avoids repetition and therefore makes writing more fluent.

Sandra had a lot of work to do so Sandra switched on Sandra's computer and opened up Sandra's document on the computer.

Sandra had a lot of work to do so <u>she</u> switched on <u>her</u> computer and opened up <u>her</u> document on <u>it</u>.

THE PRONOUNS	
I	me
you	
he	him
she	her
it	its
we	us
they	them

'I' and 'me'

Most of the pronouns have two forms. When writing, we usually use the correct form instinctively.

Give that to <u>me</u>. (not 'Give that to I')

She did that for us. (not 'we')

I went out with him. (not 'he')

Sometimes, though, the distinction is not immediately clear.

The award was given to my friend and <u>me</u>. ✓

The award was given to my friend and <u>I</u>. ✗

To decide which is correct in these situations, you should look at the sentence and deal with the two people separately. You will immediately see which is correct.

'The award was given to me' or 'The award was given to I'.

My friend and <u>I have been invited to a party</u>. ✓

My friend and <u>me have been invited to a party</u>. ✗

For more help see GCSE Success Guide page **14**

Adjectives

What are adjectives?

Adjectives are words which tell us more about nouns and pronouns.

Simon is a tall, thin, young man with dark hair and a pale face.

In this sentence, the adjectives give us more information about Simon. If the adjectives are taken out, much of the meaning of the sentence is lost ('Simon is a man with hair and a face').

Types of adjectives

Types of adjectives	Examples
Adjective of quantity	There were seven students in the show.
Adjective of quality	Our neighbour is very inquisitive.
Possessive adjective	That is my pen you are using.
Emphasising adjective	You are the very person for the job.
Interrogative adjective	Whose book is this?
Relative adjective	I know a man whose friend was a gold medallist.
Demonstrative adjective	That work is not good enough.
Exclamatory adjective	What nerve!
Adjective formed from a proper noun	the Australian team

The function of adjectives

Using well-chosen adjectives in your work can make your writing more vivid and interesting. Be selective, though, and only use adjectives which best convey to your reader the ideas or images or impression you want to create.

Beware of over-using adjectives – this can make your writing sound forced, artificial or very verbose and ornate.

For more help see GCSE Success Guide pages **14, 22**

Verbs

What are verbs?

Verbs are very important parts of speech. Without verbs, sentences are not possible.

- Verbs express **actions** – sometimes they are called 'doing' words.

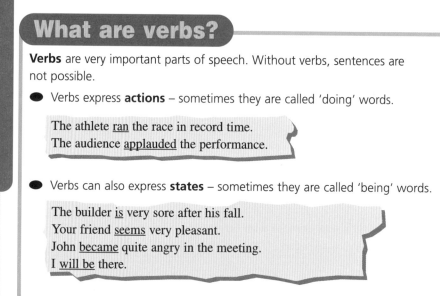

The athlete <u>ran</u> the race in record time.
The audience <u>applauded</u> the performance.

- Verbs can also express **states** – sometimes they are called 'being' words.

The builder <u>is</u> very sore after his fall.
Your friend <u>seems</u> very pleasant.
John <u>became</u> quite angry in the meeting.
I <u>will be</u> there.

Verbs and sentences

Every sentence needs a finite verb.

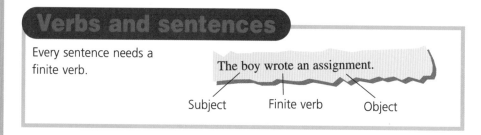

The boy wrote an assignment.

Subject   Finite verb   Object

Tenses

Tenses show when the action of the verb takes place – in the past, present or future. A change of tense is signified by the way the verb changes its ending.

PRESENT TENSE

This uses the base form of the verb which changes only in the third person singular when 's' is added to the end.

I/you/we/they <u>love</u> → he/she/it loves

PAST TENSE

The past tense is often formed by adding 'ed' to the base verb.

> I <u>walked</u>, I <u>snored</u>

However, there are verbs that do not adhere to this.

> I <u>ran</u>, I <u>went</u>

FUTURE TENSE

Unlike some other languages, English does not have a future tense ending. In English, future time is expressed by various means:

- The use of 'will' or 'shall'

> I will see you there.

- The present tense and description of 'when'.

> I leave tomorrow.

Agreement between verbs and nouns

In your writing, you should take care to match plural verbs with plural nouns and singular verbs with singular nouns.

> Each candidate <u>have</u> received their results now. ✗
> Each candidate <u>has</u> received their results now. ✓

singular noun   singular verb

> My friend <u>are</u> going away soon. ✗
> My friend <u>is</u> going away soon. ✓

singular noun   singular verb

REMEMBER

could of	would of	should of	might of ✗
could have	would have	should have	might have ✓
could've	would've	should've	might've ✓

For more help see GCSE Success Guide page 14

Adverbs

What are adverbs?

Adverbs tell us more about verbs:

● Where something happened ● How something happened

● When something happened.

They supply the extra detail we need in order to imagine or visualise the incident being described.

> He looked <u>sneeringly</u> at me.
> I ran <u>quickly</u> up the hill.

Other adverbs, such as 'rather', 'extremely', 'very', 'nearly', can be used to increase the precision of the description.

> The customer smiled <u>rather uneasily</u>.

Types of adverbs

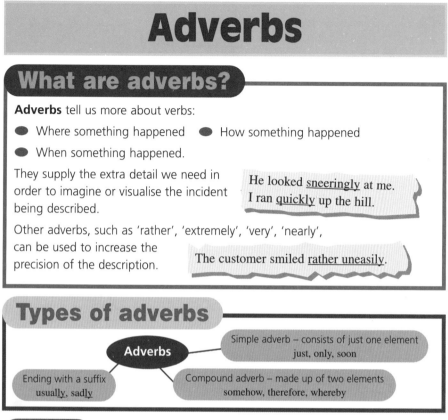

Adverbs

Simple adverb – consists of just one element
just, only, soon

Ending with a suffix
usual<u>ly</u>, sad<u>ly</u>

Compound adverb – made up of two elements
somehow, therefore, whereby

'Only'

Students sometimes have a problem with the adverb 'only'. You need to position this adverb carefully because its location in a sentence can change the meaning completely.

> Only children enjoy playing computer games.

Nobody but children enjoy playing computer games.

> Children only enjoy playing computer games.

Children don't enjoy playing anything else but computer games.

Adverbial phrases

An adverb is a single word, but sometimes several words can combine together to create an **adverbial phrase**.

> The boy sat <u>next to me</u>.
> He plays football <u>like a professional</u>.

For more help see GCSE Success Guide pages **14, 22**

What is punctuation for?

Punctuation and meaning

The main thing to remember about punctuation, is that it is there to make your writing clear and easier to understand.

When we communicate with each other using speech, we have various ways of making our words easy to understand – we pause between words, alter our tone of voice, and use facial expressions and other kinds of body language.

When we write our words down, we only have punctuation marks to help make our meaning clear.

> I started my revision this weekend did you asked Alison I started mine on Wednesday is it going well asked Luke so far

Without punctuation marks it is impossible to determine who is saying what. Here are two possible interpretations:

> 'I started my revision this weekend.'
> 'Did you?' asked Alison. 'I started mine on Wednesday.'
> 'Is it going well,' asked Luke, 'so far?'

> 'I started my revision this weekend. Did you?' asked Alison.
> 'I started mine on Wednesday. It is going well?' asked Luke.
> 'So far.'

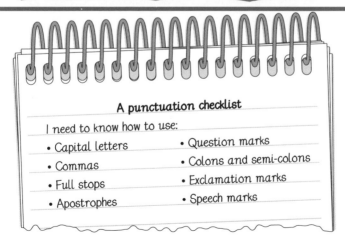

A punctuation checklist

I need to know how to use:

- Capital letters
- Commas
- Full stops
- Apostrophes
- Question marks
- Colons and semi-colons
- Exclamation marks
- Speech marks

For more help see GCSE Success Guide **pages** 6–13

Capital letters

You SHOULD use capital letters:	Example
To start the first word of a new sentence	It was a bright, cold day.
When referring to yourself	I couldn't see where I was going.
Names of people and titles	Sara, Mr. Edwards, Lord Netherborne
Places, days of the week, months and special days	Westminster Abbey, Monday, June, All Saints Day
Countries, nationalities, nations, languages, religions	Denmark, Australian, Spanish, Arabic, Christianity
Books, films and plays (first and main words only)	*The Merchant of Venice, Spider Man, One Flew Over the Cuckoo's Nest*

You SHOULD NOT use capital letters:	Example
Seasons of the year	spring, summer, autumn, winter
School subjects (excepts ones such as English, French and German)	biology, geography, maths, science, music

Capitals and meaning

Using a capital letter can be vital to make your meaning clear.

A thirteen year old girl from Birmingham was suspended by her Head for refusing to take out her nose ring.

> The girl was suspended from school by the Head teacher.

A thirteen year old girl from Birmingham was suspended by her head for refusing to take out her nose ring.

> The girl was actually suspended by her head.

Words that do begin with a capital letter

Paris	Atlantic	Wednesday
Hinduism	King Henry	
North Sea	Sweden	
December	New York	

Words that do not begin with a capital letter

country   religion   sea

autumn   month

queen (unless you a referring to a specific queen i.e 'The Queen')

For more help see GCSE Success Guide page **7**

Full stops

When to use full stops

Sentences always end with a **full stop** (or a question mark/exclamation mark functioning as a full stop).

How you divide up your writing into sentences, though, depends to a large extent on the kind of effect you want to achieve.

- Short sentences can often increase the pace of a piece of writing or give it an added sense of urgency.

> The car hurtled down the hill. The driver frantically pressed the pedal to the floor. But then he realised the brakes had failed.

- Longer sentences can slow the pace of the writing or convey more complex ideas.

> The car hurtled down the hill as the driver frantically pressed the pedal to the floor, but then he realised the brakes had failed.

Full stops or commas?

Completed statements should be separated with full stops not commas. All of the commas below should be replaced with full stops.

> It was late and the streets were deserted, when I reached my house it was all in darkness and so I assumed everyone was in bed, I fumbled in my pocket for my key.

Abbreviations

Full stops are also used to mark an abbreviation. They indicate where a word has been shortened.

B.A. → Bachelor of Arts

etc. → etcetera

It has become the norm nowadays not to use full stops with some frequently used abbreviations: GCSE, BBC, ITV, AQA.

There are also abbreviations which form words, and these do not use full stops either: NATO.

For more help see **GCSE Success Guide** page **8**

Question marks and exclamation marks

When to use a question mark

Usually it is quite clear where **question marks** should be used – a question mark should be put at the end of every sentence that asks a question. The main problem that occurs is forgetting to put them in!

When not to use a question mark

Never use a full stop and a question mark together.

Do not use a question mark if the reader/listener is expected to act instead of reply (although if the request appears too blunt as a statement, a question mark can be used).

> Will you please send me further details about your offer.
> Will you please present your report immediately?

Do not use a question mark in a sentence that asks an **indirect question**.

Indirect questions:	Direct questions:
He asked me why I was late for the lesson.	Have you change for a twenty pound note?
She wondered if I would mind giving her my phone number.	What time does the performance finish?
I asked him what he had got for his birthday.	Do you want to come in now?
The speaker asked the audience if they could hear him at the back.	How are you going to manage?
My neighbour inquired if I could help him push his car.	Could I borrow your pen please?

Exclamation marks

An **exclamation mark** should be used after a word or a group of words to show strong feeling such as:

- Anger
- Happiness
- Surprise
- Fear.

When to use exclamation marks

EMPHATIC COMMANDS

'Stop talking at once!' shouted the teacher.

VEHEMENT OR STRONGLY FELT SENTIMENTS

'God bless you, sir!' said the homeless man.

BRIEF EXPRESSIONS OF STRONG FEELING

'Help!', 'Ouch!', 'Hooray!'

If the brief exclamation is part of a longer sentence you could punctuate it in two ways:

1. You could divide it into two sentences.
    'Stop that now! Or there will be trouble.'

2. Or you could keep it as one sentence.
     'Stop that now, or there will be trouble!'

EXCLAMATORY SENTENCES
This kind of sentence usually begins with 'What', 'Where' or 'How'.

'What blue eyes you have!', 'How could you do that!', 'What a terrible day it is!'

You need to distinguish between exclamatory sentences which begin with 'What' and 'How', and questions which begin with 'What' and 'How', so pay careful attention to what the sentence says.

REMEMBER
Your choice of an exclamation mark or a question mark can alter the meaning.

Use exclamation marks sparingly – they lose their effectiveness if you over-use them.

For more help see GCSE Success Guide page **9**

QUICK REFERENCE

Commas and inverted commas

Commas

Commas are used to separate parts of a sentence and help to make it clearer.

- Always use a comma in a sentence containing two complete statements that are joined by the conjunctions 'but', 'nor' or 'for'.
- When two complete statements are joined by 'and' or 'or', the comma is optional.

Commas are used in all of the following ways.

TO SEPARATE THE PARTS OF A SENTENCE

There were many books for sale, but I couldn't find the one I was looking for.

On Saturday we saw Manchester City, my favourite team, win in the quarter final.

Auntie Hilda, who loves a glass or two of stout, sometimes drinks a little too much.

TO SEPARATE NAMES OF PEOPLE SPOKEN TO

I wonder, Mr Stables, if you have completed your plans as yet?

How many times do I need to tell you, Kate, that you must lock the back door before you go out.

TO SEPARATE ITEMS IN A LIST

The car was advertised as being complete with tow bar, sun roof, radio/cassette player, six months tax and twelve months MOT.

TO SEPARATE CONSECUTIVE ADJECTIVES

The comma replaces the word 'and'.

A tall, dark, handsome stranger stood at the door.

The plum was ripe, juicy, succulent and just asking to be eaten.

TO SEPARATE A TAG QUESTION

A **tag question** changes a statement into a question. It is always separated from the rest of the question by a comma.

His sister left school last year, <u>didn't she</u>?

TO SEPARATE WORDS SUCH AS 'YES', 'NO', 'THANK YOU'

Words and phrases like 'yes', 'no' and 'thank you' are separated in the same way as a tag question.

No, I'm afraid that is not allowed.

Yes, that is my ruler.

TO INDICATE A PAUSE OR TO AVOID CONFUSION

Whatever you do, do well.

To Jenny, Thomas remained a child.

TO SET OFF A DIRECT QUOTATION FROM THE REST OF THE SENTENCE

'Come in out of the rain,' said Timothy.

'I can't. I haven't finished yet,' said Alice.

Inverted commas

AROUND THE TITLES OF BOOKS, NEWSPAPERS, FILMS, ETC.

I bought a copy of 'The Mirror' and 'The Guardian' in order to compare their stories.

We are studying 'Romeo and Juliet' for our GCSE English course.

Note: In print, the inverted commas are often left out and the words appear in italic type.

AROUND QUOTATIONS

The use of inverted commas in this respect is very similar to the way they are used in speech punctuation.

One of my favourite speeches from 'Hamlet' begins, 'To be, or not to be,' but another well known one begins, 'Alas, poor Yorick. I knew him, Horatio.'

TO STRESS OR EMPHASISE A PARTICULAR WORD OR PHRASE

How do you spell 'onomatopoeia'?

'Understanding' is not the word I would use to describe him.

SINGLE OR DOUBLE?

Either single or double inverted commas are correct, but you should be consistent. Chose one method and stick to it throughout your work.

For more help see GCSE Success Guide pages 10–11

Apostrophes

What are apostrophes for?

Apostrophes are used for two purposes:

● They can be used for shortening words (shortened words are called 'contractions').

● They can be used to indicate possession.

Contractions

This use of the apostrophe is quite straightforward.

● An apostrophe shows that one or more letters have been missed out.

I can't do this work.→ I cannot do this work.
I'll try to help you. → I will try to help you.

● An apostrophe is always used when writing the time.

It is nearly four o'clock. → It is nearly four of the clock.

● An apostrophe is also used in a contraction to indicate the missing out of numbers.

23 September '04

Do not use apostrophes for: his, hers, our, yours, theirs

The possessive apostrophe

This use of an apostrophe shows that someone owns something, and it is probably the most misused of all the punctuation marks. It is quite straightforward to use, though, if you stick to the following rules:

● If only one person owns something use **'s** (apostrophe first).

David's bike (the bike belonging to David) was quite new.
The leather on Kate's new briefcase (the briefcase belonging to Kate) was very stiff.

- If more than one person owns something use **s'** (apostrophe second).

  The boys' house stood in its own grounds.
  The girls' coats had been stolen.

- If two or more people are named then use **'s** (apostrophe first) on the last name only.

  Tim, Rachael and Neil's new school suited them very well.

- Some words have special plurals that do not end in s (men, women, geese, mice, children). With these words, always use **'s** (apostrophe first).

  The men's changing room was very cold.
  The children's art lesson was cancelled.

A checklist of possessive apostrophe rules

Singular nouns ⟶ always need 's

the woman's car
the dog's food

Plural nouns which are formed by adding s ⟶ always need s'

the dogs' food

Plural nouns which are irregular and do not end in s ⟶ always need 's

the women's cars
the geese's pen

Colons and semi-colons

What are they for?

Often, students are very unsure about how to use **colons** and **semi-colons** correctly. They tend to be used less in written English than they used to be, but they do still have a very clear function to perform.

Colons to introduce lists

You will need to bring the following items:
a sleeping bag, food, a change of clothes, sun block, a bat, stout boots.

For this recipe you will need the following ingredients:
sugar, flour, milk, butter.

These are the books you will need: 'Macbeth', 'To Kill a Mockingbird', 'The Dead Sea Poems'.

Make sure that you have some kind of introductory phrase before the colon.

Colons to punctuate dialogue in plays

Colons are used in drama scripts to separate each character from their speech.

The Inspector: Don't stammer and yammer at me, man!

Colons before direct speech

Sometimes a writer uses colons instead of commas before direct speech in narrative (this is less usual than the comma though).

Running back he shouted: 'Keep going!'

For more help see GCSE Success Guide page 8

More examples of the colon in use

- I checked I had all the tools I needed: a saw, screwdriver, chisel, hammer and pincers.
- Kate enjoyed a variety of school subjects: English, history, French, maths, geography and art.
- Listen carefully and then do the following: go into the library; select the book you want; take it to the desk; give it to the librarian.
- There are several things on my list: a digital camera; DVD player; BMX bike; new watch and a pair of trainers.

Semi-colons to join two sentences

Semi-colons can be used to join together two sentences that are closely related in meaning.

He had a very late night. He was late for work.

Clearly these two sentences are closely related.

He had a very late night; he was late for work.

The two sentences can be re-written as one using a semi-colon.

Note that only complete sentences can be joined in this way and they must be linked in meaning.

Semi-colons to separate items in a list

Semi-colons can be used to replace commas in a list, particularly if the items are lengthy and if they already contain commas.

Every student should bring the following items: a lightweight, waterproof coat, waterproof over-trousers, a thick, warm fleece, woolly socks, waterproof, thick-soled walking boots, packed lunch.

This is quite confusing.

Every student should bring the following items: a lightweight, waterproof coat; waterproof over-trousers; a thick, warm fleece; woolly socks; waterproof, thick-soled walking boots; packed lunch.

Semi-colons make things much clearer.

Speech punctuation

Rules for using speech marks

Direct speech is writing down what somebody said using the exact words that they used. Here are some simple rules to follow when using speech marks:

- Speech marks enclose everything that is actually said.
- The first set of speech marks goes at the beginning of the first words spoken.
- The second set of speech marks goes after the punctuation at the ends of the words spoken.

> The term **speech marks** here means exactly the same as **inverted commas** or **quotation marks**.

The man said, 'It is very wet today.'

Different speech mark patterns

There are four sentence patterns that direct speech can follow.

1. Narrative → speech

The teacher said, 'Stop writing and put your pens down.'

In this pattern of speech punctuation:

- There is always a comma marking the transition from narrative to speech.
- The speech marks enclose the words spoken and the final full stop (or question mark or exclamation mark).
- The first word of the direct speech always begins with a capital letter. This word is the first word of the spoken sentence and, as you know, the first word of a sentence always begins with a capital letter.

2. Speech → narrative

'Close your books and listen carefully,' she told us.

In this pattern of speech punctuation:

- There is always a comma, a question mark or an exclamation mark marking the change from speech to narrative.
- The speech marks enclose both the words that are spoken and the punctuation marks that go with them.

3. Speech → narrative → same sentence of speech continues

> 'Don't go that way,' said the guide, 'or you may get lost.'

This pattern of speech punctuation puts together the two patterns we have already seen:

● Notice how 'or' in the example begins with a small letter. This is because the sentence of direct speech has not ended yet.

4. Speech → narrative → new sentence of speech

> 'Get out your map and look carefully for the nearest village,' said our leader. 'When you have found it, calculate how long it will take us to get there.'

In this pattern of speech punctuation:

● One pair of speech marks enclose the speech that comes before the narration, and one pair encloses the part afterwards.
● The narration ends with a full stop and the new sentence of speech begins with a capital letter.

More than one speaker

When more than one person is speaking, every time a new person (or someone different from the last speaker) begins to speak, you should start a new line.

> 'Hello,' said John.
> 'Hi,' replied Karen. 'I'm sorry I'm late. Have you been waiting long?'
> 'No, I've only just arrived.'
> 'Good. Let's go then,' said Karen.

Note here how John's reply to Karen's question does not tell you who is speaking. Sometimes it is not necessary to say who speaks every word as the context will tell you who is speaking.

REMEMBER

Never use speech marks when writing playscripts.

For more help see GCSE Success Guide pages **10–11**

Spellings

How to avoid common mistakes

Some of the most common mistakes that students make in their written work are to do with spelling. These mistakes are usually made for a particular reason. Here are some of the most common problems:

- Missing a letter out

  adress instead of address
  accomodate rather than accommodate

- Getting letters the wrong way round

  decieve instead of deceive

- Putting a letter in

  sherriff instead of sheriff
  dissappoint instead of disappoint

- Spelling a word as it is said

  busness instead of business

- Confusing two words

  there/their/they're
  quiet/quite, accept/except, weather/whether

Some simple rules

- 'i' before 'e' except after 'c' when the sound is 'ee'

  believe, thief, chief, grief, ceiling, perceive, receive, receipt

- Words spelt 'ei' – the sound is **not** 'ee'

  rein, feign, veil, neighbour, height, weight, their, reign, eight

- Words ending in 'l' and adding 'ly' have 'lly'

  faithful → faithfully
  beautiful → beautifully

- Words ending in 'y' change the 'y' to an 'i' when 'ly' is added

  happy → happily
  pretty → prettily

  Except shy → shyly, sly → slyly

- Nouns ending in 'y' drop the 'y' and add 'ies' in the plural

  fifty → fifties
  factory → factories

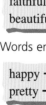

Words ending in a silent 'e' drop the 'e' when an ending is added that starts with a vowel.

hate → hating
have → having
love → lovable

Words ending in a silent 'e' do not drop the 'e' when an ending is added that starts with a consonant.

like → likely
fate → fateful

Except true → truly, due → duly

Words ending in 'ge' and 'ce' keep the 'e' when an ending is added.

change → changeable
notice → noticeable
advantage → advantageous

Confusing endings

Common errors often occur because of confusion in the word endings. Some of the most common ones are:

- '...ant' and '...ent'

  dependant, dependent, independent

- '...ance' and '...ence'

  perseverance, transference

- '...er' and '...or'

  predecessor, category, register

- '...able' and '...ible'

  irresistible, predictable

- '...er' and '...ar'

  secretary, stationary, stationery

For more help see GCSE Success Guide pages 16–19

Planning

What is narrative writing?

As part of your GCSE English course, you will need to write to 'explore, imagine and entertain', often by writing a story of some kind. This is sometimes called **narrative writing**.

Writing a story sounds like a simple task, but writing an effective story needs careful planning and there are a number of elements to think about.

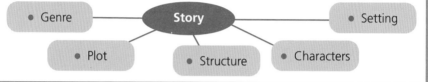

- Genre
- Story
- Setting
- Plot
- Structure
- Characters

Planning a story

1. Decide on the **genre** of your story, e.g. detective story, love story, science fiction, adventure.

2. Decide on the **narrative viewpoint**.

4. Structure the events of your plot into order. Remember that an effective story has:
- An effective opening which captures the reader's attention
- Interesting developments, often with a climax
- A satisfying end.

3. Write down ideas for the **plot** or storyline. Some people begin by thinking of their characters and then base the story around them. Others like to think of the storyline first and then create the characters to fit their storyline.

5. Make brief notes on the **characters**. Aim to create a small number of well-developed characters.

6. Decide on the **setting** for your story. Make sure that your setting is believable and convincing.

For more help see GCSE Success Guide pages 32–33

Beginnings and endings

Starting the story

Often, making a start on the story itself can be the hardest part. It is very important that the opening captures the reader's attention and makes him/her want to read on.

There are various ways that you can make the opening of your story lively, interesting and effective.

Options for beginnings

Give your reader information about the character, background or setting.

Plunge your reader straight into the story by opening with a dramatic event. You can then fill in background information later as the plot develops.

Start with some kind of event or conversation which is puzzling or intriguing and raises your reader's curiosity.

Begin with some dialogue between characters.

Ending the story

The ending of the story is as important as the opening. There are various ways in which you can end your story. Think carefully about which is most effective for your particular story.

Options for endings

The ending can develop naturally from what has happened – the plot draws to a natural conclusion.

End with a dramatic or exciting event.

The ending could be full of suspense to keep the reader's attention right up to the end.

There could be an unexpected twist at the end.

The ending could reveal information or sort out confusions for the reader.

The ending could reveal some kind of moral or message.

For more help see GCSE Success Guide pages **32–33**

Creating characters

How to make up characters

Characters are a key element in any story. Characters – whether they are humans, animals or even aliens from space – need to be created from your imagination.

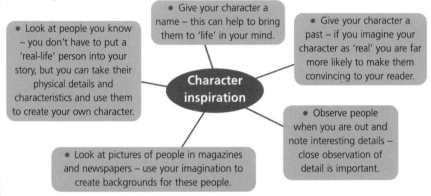

- Look at people you know – you don't have to put a 'real-life' person into your story, but you *can* take their physical details and characteristics and use them to create your own character.

- Give your character a name – this can help to bring them to 'life' in your mind.

- Give your character a past – if you imagine your character as 'real' you are far more likely to make them convincing to your reader.

Character inspiration

- Observe people when you are out and note interesting details – close observation of detail is important.

- Look at pictures of people in magazines and newspapers – use your imagination to create backgrounds for these people.

How many characters should there be?

You can spoil a good plot by including too many characters. Your story is going to be quite short and so you can only develop a small number of characters. You shouldn't try to have more than one main character and two or three other important characters.

How to reveal characters to the reader

- **Description** – give details of the character either in a particular section or as the narrative develops.

- **Dialogue** – you can reveal a lot through what your characters say and what others say about them.

- **Thoughts and feelings** – what is going on 'inside' a character can be revealed directly, particularly in a first-person narrative.

- **Actions and reactions** – details can be revealed through what your characters do and how they behave in various situations.

For more help see **GCSE Success Guide** page **32**

Describing a scene or setting

Create a setting for your characters

Your characters do not operate in a vacuum – they move within a **scene** or **setting** that you create. Your scene or setting must be just as convincing as your characters.

Atmosphere is closely connected to the setting you create.

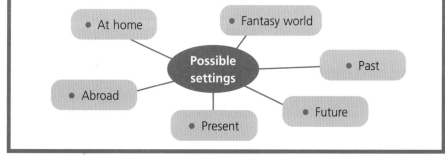

- At home
- Fantasy world
- **Possible settings**
- Past
- Abroad
- Future
- Present

How to reveal setting to the reader

Creating a successful setting involves careful use of descriptive language. But you will also need to decide at which point in the plot to include that description. How you write about your setting will depend on the type of story you are creating.

- You can suggest the setting through small touches of detail as you develop the plot.
- You could give more detailed description, perhaps a paragraph or section setting the scene.
- You could allow an impression of the scene or setting to emerge indirectly, perhaps through the dialogue of the characters.

REMEMBER

Avoid over-elaborate description. This can make your story sound forced and therefore unconvincing.

For more help see GCSE Success Guide page 32

Non-fiction writing

What is non-fiction?

The term 'non-fiction' covers a wide range of types of writing.

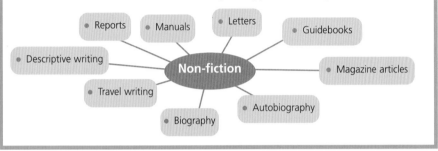

- Reports
- Manuals
- Letters
- Guidebooks
- Descriptive writing
- **Non-fiction**
- Magazine articles
- Travel writing
- Autobiography
- Biography

Planning a non-fiction assignment

Follow these steps when creating a non-fiction piece.

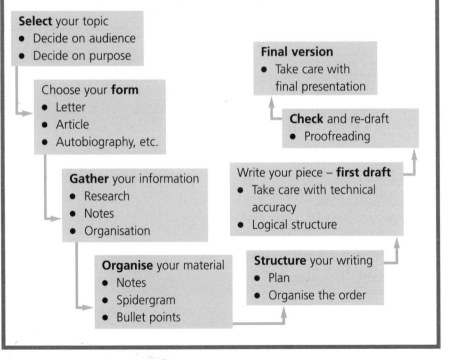

Select your topic
- Decide on audience
- Decide on purpose

Choose your **form**
- Letter
- Article
- Autobiography, etc.

Gather your information
- Research
- Notes
- Organisation

Organise your material
- Notes
- Spidergram
- Bullet points

Structure your writing
- Plan
- Organise the order

Write your piece – **first draft**
- Take care with technical accuracy
- Logical structure

Check and re-draft
- Proofreading

Final version
- Take care with final presentation

For more help see **GCSE Success Guide** pages **34–35**

Informative writing

What is informative writing?

The main **purpose** of informative writing is to put across information to the reader as clearly and effectively as possible.

Information can come in many forms.

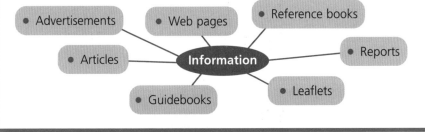

- Advertisements
- Web pages
- Reference books
- Articles
- **Information**
- Reports
- Guidebooks
- Leaflets

Features of informative writing

Whatever their purpose and audience, all informative texts have a number of features in common. Informative writing:

- Uses language clearly
- Focuses on its purpose
- Is aimed at a particular audience
- Gives the reader specific information
- May use photographs, illustrations, etc. to make the information clearer.

Planning informative writing

1. Identify your **audience** and **purpose**.

2. List the **key points** you want to put across to your reader.

3. **Structure** them in a logical way.

4. Decide on the level of **detail** you want to include.

5. Plan your method of **presentation**.

6. Make sure your information is clear and **easy to understand**.

For more help see GCSE Success Guide pages **92–93**

Writing to explain

What is writing to explain?

There is some degree of overlap between writing to explain and writing to inform, but there is a difference between the two.

When writing to explain, your **purpose** is to make something clear to your reader. It often addresses the questions: What? How? Why?

Writing to explain can take a variety of forms depending on its purpose.

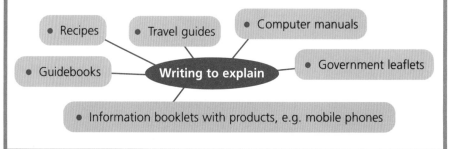

- Recipes
- Travel guides
- Computer manuals
- Guidebooks
- **Writing to explain**
- Government leaflets
- Information booklets with products, e.g. mobile phones

Features of explanatory writing

Explanatory writing should be:

- Clearly and logically structured
- Concise
- Presented visually in a form that makes it easier to understand.

Planning explanatory writing

1. Be aware of your **purpose** and **audience**.

2. List the **details** to be included.

3. Structure them into a logical order.

4. Make sure your **language** is clear and straightforward.

5. Make sure there is **no ambiguity** or any unclear points in your explanation.

For more help see GCSE Success Guide pages **92–93**

Analytical writing

What is analytical writing?

The analytical writing task you might be asked to do as part of your GCSE English course can take a number of forms.

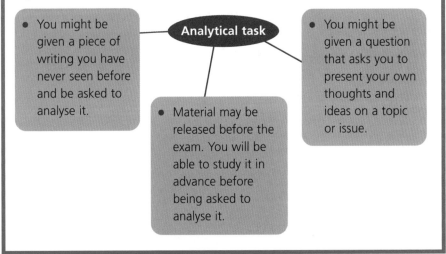

- You might be given a piece of writing you have never seen before and be asked to analyse it.

Analytical task

- Material may be released before the exam. You will be able to study it in advance before being asked to analyse it.

- You might be given a question that asks you to present your own thoughts and ideas on a topic or issue.

Features of analytical writing

All analytical tasks require the following skills:

- A clear communication of ideas
- An awareness of the way writing is used for a specific purpose and audience
- The ability to examine language and its effects
- The presentation of ideas in a clear and logical way.

How to analyse

- Examine the content, ideas and issues that the text explores.
- Investigate the ways in which language is used to express ideas and the effects that it creates.
- Consider your own thoughts and ideas on the topic or issue.

For more help see **GCSE Success Guide** pages **90–91**

Writing about newspapers

Useful terms when writing about

NEWSPAPERS

banner – a front page headline that runs across the top of the page

caption – the words that explain photographs or illustrations

column – vertical section of text

copy – the written material that reporters submit for publishing

editorial – a column in which the newspaper expresses its opinion on a topic

exclusive – a story only covered by one newspaper

eye-witness report – where a reporter was actually at the scene

feature – a special, usually longer news story

filler – a short article used to fill space

hard news – news that focuses on factual detail

headline – the main heading on an article or report

human interest story – an article, usually focused on one person, which relates an emotional event/ story, such as tragedy, success, failure, achievement

in-depth reporting – covers a topic or issue in detail

lead – the main story on the page

punch-line – the main point of the story

soft news – a light news story

What's in a newspaper?

As part of your course, you will need to analyse and write about **media texts**. The main kinds of media texts you are likely to encounter are articles and reports from newspapers.

The primary **purpose** of newspapers is to report news, but they also contain a lot of other material as well.

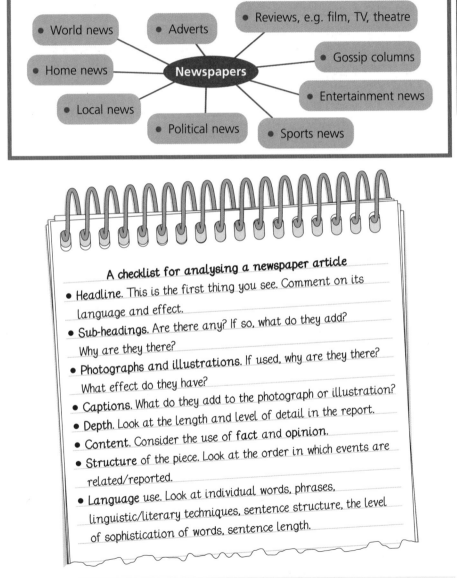

- World news
- Adverts
- Reviews, e.g. film, TV, theatre
- Home news
- Newspapers
- Gossip columns
- Local news
- Entertainment news
- Political news
- Sports news

A checklist for analysing a newspaper article

- **Headline.** This is the first thing you see. Comment on its language and effect.
- **Sub-headings.** Are there any? If so, what do they add? Why are they there?
- **Photographs and illustrations.** If used, why are they there? What effect do they have?
- **Captions.** What do they add to the photograph or illustration?
- **Depth.** Look at the length and level of detail in the report.
- **Content.** Consider the use of fact and opinion.
- **Structure** of the piece. Look at the order in which events are related/reported.
- **Language** use. Look at individual words, phrases, linguistic/literary techniques, sentence structure, the level of sophistication of words, sentence length.

For more help see GCSE Success Guide pages 38–42

Analysing advertisements

What is an advertisement?

In your English exam you may be given an **advertisement** to write about.

Advertising can take many forms (see below) but the **purpose** is always the same: to persuade. Adverts are designed to persuade the audience to behave or think in a particular way. The audience can vary depending on the particular advert.

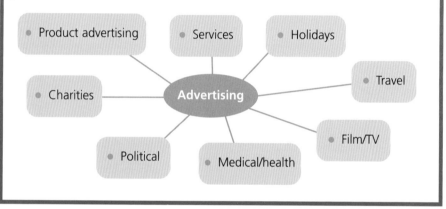

- Product advertising
- Services
- Holidays
- Charities
- **Advertising**
- Travel
- Political
- Medical/health
- Film/TV

The language of advertising

Adverts can use a whole range of language techniques:

- Exaggeration
- Imperatives
- Claims which cannot be proved (or disproved)
- Repetition
- Appealing words
- Words that create 'sound' effects
- Words that appeal to taste
- Imagery
- Technical or scientific (or pseudo-scientific vocabulary)
- Puns (plays on words)
- Humorous language
- Emotive language.

What makes an advert effective?

The target audience

Who is the advert aimed at? This will have a major influence on content, layout, presentation and use of stereotypes.

The appeal

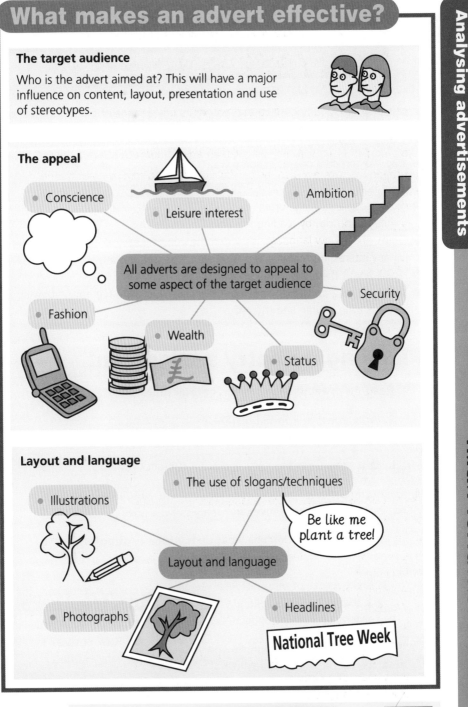

- Conscience
- Leisure interest
- Ambition
- Security
- Fashion
- Wealth
- Status

All adverts are designed to appeal to some aspect of the target audience

Layout and language

- The use of slogans/techniques

Be like me plant a tree!

- Illustrations
- Photographs

Layout and language

- Headlines

National Tree Week

For more help see GCSE Success Guide pages 42–43

Studying poetry

Poetry and your GCSE

As part of your GCSE English course, you will study a range of poems, including those from different cultures and traditions. If you are studying GCSE English Literature, you will study both pre-1914 and post-1914 poetry and you will also be asked to compare poems in some way.

Here are some ideas to help you prepare yourself for studying poetry:

- Poems come in many forms. You should become familiar with as wide a range as you can by reading lots of different poems.
- Think about how language is used in the poems you read and make a note of any interesting features, e.g. striking images, interesting lines or words.
- Think about the ideas in the poems you read.
- Read poems aloud when you can – this helps you get a feel for features such as tone, rhyme and rhythm.

Planning a poetry assignment

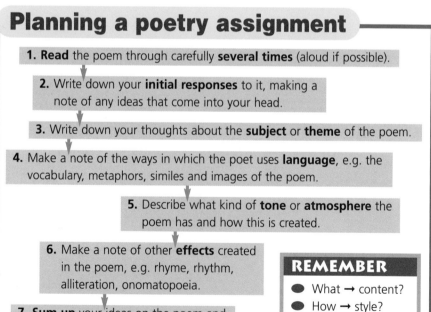

1. Read the poem through carefully **several times** (aloud if possible).

2. Write down your **initial responses** to it, making a note of any ideas that come into your head.

3. Write down your thoughts about the **subject** or **theme** of the poem.

4. Make a note of the ways in which the poet uses **language**, e.g. the vocabulary, metaphors, similes and images of the poem.

5. Describe what kind of **tone** or **atmosphere** the poem has and how this is created.

6. Make a note of other **effects** created in the poem, e.g. rhyme, rhythm, alliteration, onomatopoeia.

REMEMBER
- What → content?
- How → style?
- Why → effect?

7. Sum up your ideas on the poem and how the poem 'works' as a whole.

For more help see **GCSE Success Guide** pages **62–75**

Imagery

What is imagery?

It is likely that the poetry you study will use **imagery** of one kind or another.

The imagery is created through descriptive language. It helps us to clearly and vividly imagine the thing that is being described.

Images can work in different ways:

- A **literal image** re-creates the scene or description through precise language.
- **Figurative language** uses comparisons to make the description more vivid. This kind of imagery can take a variety of forms.

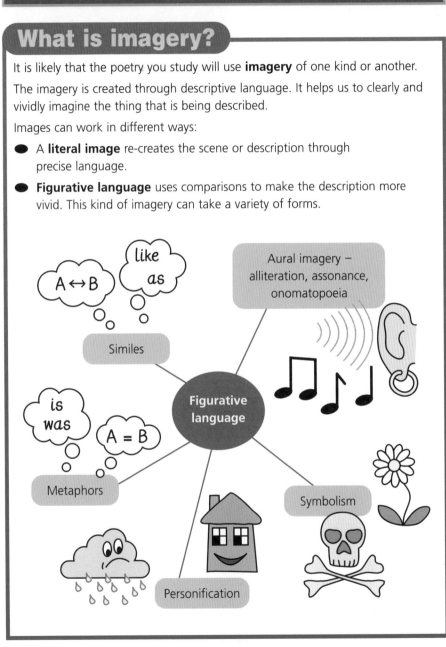

For more help see GCSE Success Guide pages 62–75

Similes, metaphors and personification

Similes

Similes are easy to spot in poetry because they compare one thing to another in order to make the description more vivid. They often use the word 'like' or 'as' to make the comparison.

The north wind cut through us like a knife.

The coldness of the north wind is compared to the action of a knife – this emphasises the sharp, penetrating nature of the wind.

Metaphors

Metaphors also create a comparison, but are less direct and don't use 'like' or 'as'.

He is a lion in battle.

The soldier is described as simply being a lion.

Personification

Personification is another form of imagery, this time created by giving human qualities or feelings to something that is not human.

The river glideth at his own sweet will.

This suggests that the river is a living, thinking being who has a will of his own.

REMEMBER

Make sure you can identify similes, metaphors and personification. When you analyse a poem, it is more important to be able to **explain the effects** that the techniques create. How do they make the description more vivid?

For more help see GCSE Success Guide pages 62–75

Aural imagery

What is aural imagery?

Some kinds of imagery create an impression through 'sound effects' rather than by creating a picture in the reader's mind. This is called **aural imagery**. Sometimes, effects are achieved through a combination of different kinds of images.

There are three main types of aural imagery that you might identify in the poems you study. These are explained below.

Alliteration

Alliteration involves the repetition of the same

> O let them be left, wildness and wet;
> Long live the weeds and the wilderness yet.

consonant sound, usually at the beginning of each word.

The repeated 'w' sound creates a sense of the sound of the wind blowing and helps to create an impression of uncultivated desolation.

Assonance

Assonance is similar to alliteration but involves the

> Shark, breathing beneath the sea,
> Has no belief, commits no treason.

repetition of a vowel sound to achieve a particular effect.

Onomatopoeia

Onomatopoeia is when the sound of a word reflects its meaning.

> The banging of the door and the
> thudding of his feet woke her up.

REMEMBER

Make sure that you can spot these features. But it is more important to **explain** why you think a poet has used them and what **effects** they create in the poem and in the mind of the reader.

For more help see GCSE Success Guide pages 62–75

Rhyme and rhythm

Rhythm

Rhythm can exert a strong influence on the overall effect of a poem, giving it a feeling of 'movement' and life. The poet can use rhythm to emphasise a certain idea in the poem or to help create its mood or tone. There are many kinds of rhythm in poetry: gentle and flowing, harsh or discordant, stilted and uneven in phrasing or regular in tempo. Poetry can have a rhythm that reflects a serious or solemn or dignified mood, or a rhythm that suggests the comic or absurd.

Poets can create and use rhythmical effects in their poetry in various ways.

- **Syllable stress** – words contain their own rhythm patterns in the sense that we stress certain syllables more than others in words when we pronounce them. Poets often use the natural rhythms within the words themselves to help contribute to the overall effect.

- **Emphatic stress** – sometimes the poet might place an emphasis on a particular word or phrase in order to achieve a particular effect.

- **Phrasing and punctuation** – the rhythm of a poem can be influenced by factors such as length of phrases, lines or sentences, the placing of punctuation marks, line breaks, stanza breaks and repetitions.

- **Metre** – technically speaking, the whole notion of rhythm in poetry is closely tied up with the idea of metre – the stress patterns used in a poem. Often poetry follows a regular rhythm pattern, but sometimes poets use irregular patterns to create particular effects. Modern poems are less likely to have strict, regular rhythm patterns than pre-1914 poems.

REMEMBER

Being able to identify the metrical pattern of a poem, or its rhyme scheme, is of little value in itself. The key thing is that you are able to say what it contributes to the **effect** of the poem overall. Ask yourself: 'Why has the poet used rhyme and rhythm in this way and what does it contribute, together with all the other features, to the overall impact of the poem?'

Rhyme

Rhyme makes an important contribution to the 'musical quality' of a poem, and can affect the sound and therefore the overall impact of the piece. The system of rhyme within a poem is called the **rhyme scheme** and it can influence the effect of a poem in a variety of ways. Although most rhymes work on the basis of the rhyme occurring at the end of a line, some occur in the middle of the line. These are called **internal rhymes**.

Working out the rhyme scheme is quite straightforward. Each line is given a letter of the alphabet starting with A. When two or more lines rhyme, they are given the same letter.

Here are some examples of traditional forms and patterns.

- **Couplets** – these are pairs of lines that rhyme (AA).

- **Triplets** – lines rhyme in sets of three (AAA).

- **Quatrains** – lines rhyming in sets of four (usual rhyme schemes are ABAB, ABCB, AAAA, ABBA, AAAB, AABA).

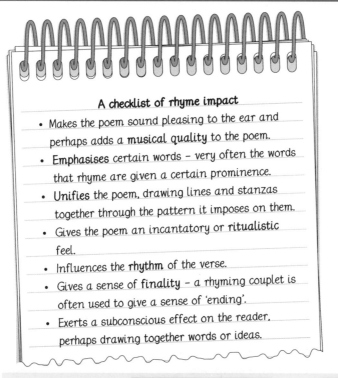

A checklist of rhyme impact

- Makes the poem sound pleasing to the ear and perhaps adds a musical quality to the poem.
- Emphasises certain words – very often the words that rhyme are given a certain prominence.
- Unifies the poem, drawing lines and stanzas together through the pattern it imposes on them.
- Gives the poem an incantatory or ritualistic feel.
- Influences the rhythm of the verse.
- Gives a sense of finality – a rhyming couplet is often used to give a sense of 'ending'.
- Exerts a subconscious effect on the reader, perhaps drawing together words or ideas.

For more help see GCSE Success Guide **pages** 62–75

Pre-1914 poetry

Social, cultural and historical context

Often, when studying pre-1914 poetry, the background to the poem can be particularly important. It consists of three main elements.

- **Social context**

| The kind of society that existed when the poem was written | ➤ | The way the theme, setting, characters of the poems are influenced by the social background |

- **Cultural context**

| The ideas, philosophies, cultural ideas that existed when the poem was written | ➤ | The beliefs, behaviour, interests, attitudes of people at the time the poem was written |

- **Historical context**

| The historical period that the poem was written in | ➤ | Events, discoveries, etc. that were important and influential in that period |

Features of pre-1914 poetry

- Some of the language used might be archaic (containing old-fashioned words that we might not understand nowadays).

- The poem might deal with ideas or themes that relate to the time when it was written.

- The poem might contain references to events, people, beliefs and attitudes that meant something to the reader when the poem was written but now are hard to understand. You will have to research these.

- The poetic style might be unusual or unfamiliar.

Poetic form

There are particular poetic forms which frequently occur in pre-1914 poetry:

- The **sonnet**
- The **ballad**
- The **elegy**.

For more help see **GCSE Success Guide** pages **62–75**

Post-1914 poetry

Modern poetic technique

Modern poetry can use the same techniques as pre-1914 poetry. In addition, it might:

- Deal with aspects of modern life and life experiences
- Make use of free verse, i.e. verse without a regular rhythm pattern and/or rhyme scheme
- Use less formal language, sometimes containing modern colloquialisms or vocabulary.

Planning a modern poetry assignment

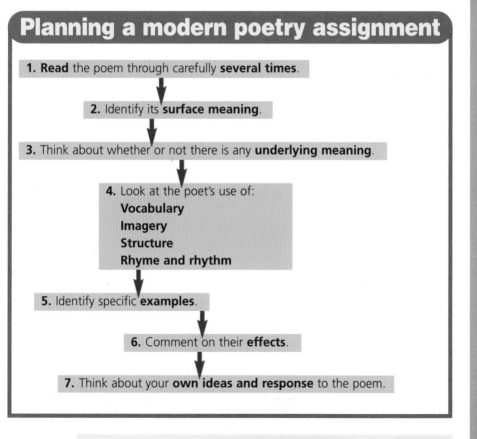

1. Read the poem through carefully **several times**.

2. Identify its **surface meaning**.

3. Think about whether or not there is any **underlying meaning**.

4. Look at the poet's use of:
   Vocabulary
   Imagery
   Structure
   Rhyme and rhythm

5. Identify specific **examples**.

6. Comment on their **effects**.

7. Think about your **own ideas and response** to the poem.

For more help see GCSE Success Guide pages **62–75**

Poetry from other cultures

How is it different?

Here are some unique features that poetry from other cultures might contain:

- Non-standard English forms
- Dialect forms of the particular culture
- Colloquial language using words of a particular culture
- Specific references relating to a particular culture
- Themes and issues that are of particular concern to the culture
- The setting might be that of a particular country or society
- The metaphors, similes and symbols that the poet uses might relate to the particular culture.

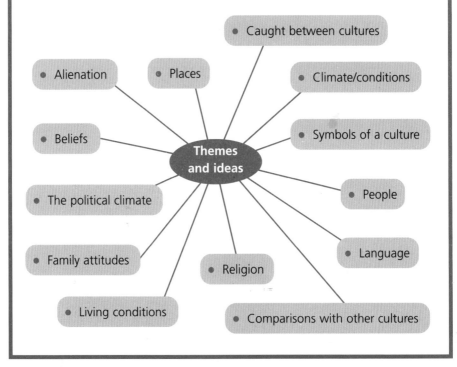

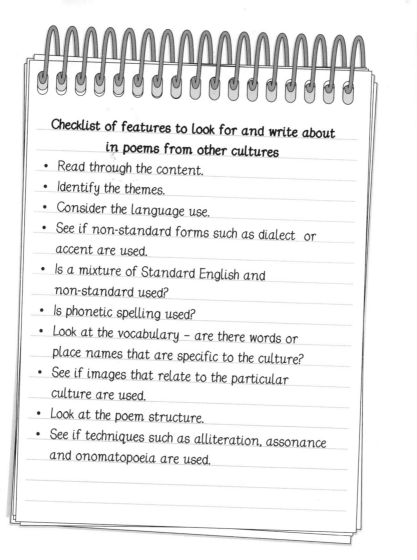

Checklist of features to look for and write about
in poems from other cultures

- Read through the content.
- Identify the themes.
- Consider the language use.
- See if non-standard forms such as dialect or
  accent are used.
- Is a mixture of Standard English and
  non-standard used?
- Is phonetic spelling used?
- Look at the vocabulary – are there words or
  place names that are specific to the culture?
- See if images that relate to the particular
  culture are used.
- Look at the poem structure.
- See if techniques such as alliteration, assonance
  and onomatopoeia are used.

REMEMBER

The important thing is not to simply identify or 'spot' features – you must
explain and analyse the effects created by the ways in which the poets
use language.

For more help see **GCSE Success Guide** pages **72–75**

Comparing poems

Comparison assignments

As part of your course, you might be required to compare two poems. You might be asked to compare:

- One modern poem with another modern poem by a different poet
- One post-1914 poem with one pre-1914 poem
- Two pre-1914 poems by different poets
- Two poems from other cultures.

When comparing poems, you should look for all the features you look for when studying a single poem.

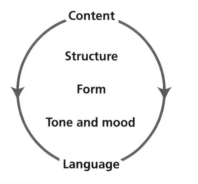

Content

Structure

Form

Tone and mood

Language

Planning your response

- **Read** both poems through carefully **several times**.

- Form an **initial impression** of each poem's themes, language use and structure.

- Note down a brief **quotation** from each poem that you will use to support your ideas.

- Make two lists – one headed **similarities** and one headed **differences** – and list key points of each poem under the appropriate headings.

Writing your response

● **Introduction** – an introductory paragraph commenting on the general themes, ideas or content of each poem.

● **Main body** – several paragraphs containing your main comparative analysis of the poems. Make your comparison integrated by making a point about poem A and then poem B and so on. Structure your ideas carefully in this section. You might have a paragraph comparing the structure of each poem, another on each poem's use of imagery, etc.

● **Conclusion** – a concluding paragraph summing up the main similarities and differences.

A checklist of integration phrases

Use these phrases to help move the analysis smoothly from poem to poem:

In comparison with ...

On the other hand ...

However ...

Compared with ...

In contrast to ...

Unlike ...

Similarly ...

Another difference/similarity ...

REMEMBER

When you answer comparison questions…

Do not write all about one poem and then all about the other.

Do not write about one poem, then the other, and then tag on a brief final paragraph where you compare them.

Integrate!

For more help see **GCSE Success Guide** pages **66–67**

Shakespeare assignments

The work you do on a play by Shakespeare for your GCSE course will be assessed against criteria that measure your ability to read and understand the material. This ability will be assessed through written responses to the play.

In studying your play you will be expected to understand:

- The **plot** of the play
- How the **characters** are presented
- The **themes** the play explores
- The ways in which **language** is used in the play
- The **dramatic techniques** and use of stagecraft
- The historical and philosophical **context** of the play
- The effect on the **audience**.

REMEMBER

Always be aware that you are studying a play and that it is meant to be seen on the stage rather than read as a text. If you can, see a performance of the play you are studying – either at the theatre or on film. This will help your understanding enormously.

Approaching your play

Be aware of the kind of play you are studying. There are four basic kinds:

- **Tragedies** – these plays focus on a tragic hero (or a couple in the case of *Romeo and Juliet*) whose downfall is brought about through misfortune or a flaw in their character. The play ends in the death of the main character, although other characters also die as a result of the tragedy.
- **Comedies** – these plays involve humour, confusion, disguise, mistaken identity, etc. and end happily.
- **Histories** – these are based on historical events and characters.
- **Romances** – these often involve magical worlds, strange events and end happily.

A checklist for effective Shakespeare study

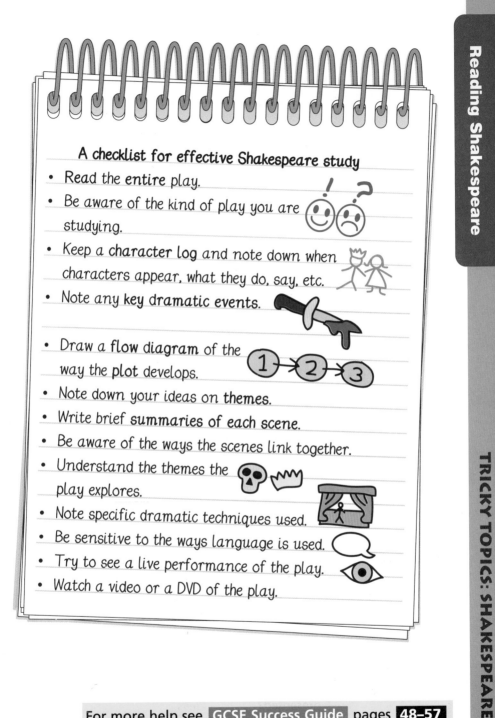

- Read the entire play.
- Be aware of the kind of play you are studying.
- Keep a **character log** and note down when characters appear, what they do, say, etc.
- Note any key **dramatic events**.
- Draw a **flow diagram** of the way the **plot** develops.
- Note down your ideas on **themes**.
- Write brief **summaries of each scene**.
- Be aware of the ways the scenes link together.
- Understand the themes the play explores.
- Note specific dramatic techniques used.
- Be sensitive to the ways language is used.
- Try to see a live performance of the play.
- Watch a video or a DVD of the play.

For more help see **GCSE Success Guide** pages **48–57**

Analysing a Shakespeare play

Key features of the play

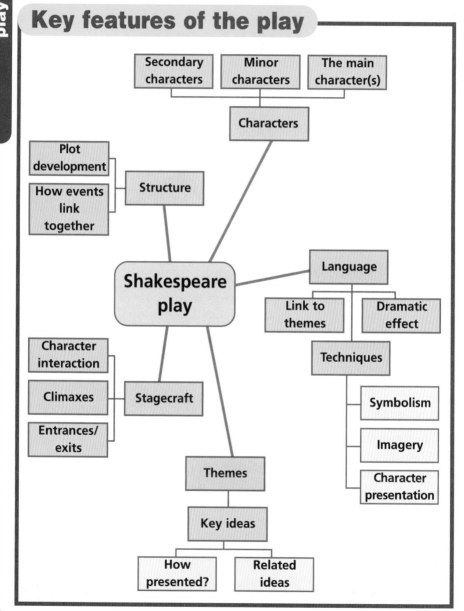

Secondary characters

Minor characters

The main character(s)

Characters

Plot development

How events link together

Structure

Shakespeare play

Language

Link to themes

Dramatic effect

Techniques

Character interaction

Climaxes

Entrances/ exits

Stagecraft

Symbolism

Imagery

Character presentation

Themes

Key ideas

How presented?

Related ideas

REMEMBER

You may only be asked to analyse one aspect of the play, such as the presentation of characters or themes, but often these cannot be discussed in isolation. Make sure you demonstrate awareness of the whole play.

The structure of your play

Before analysing the play in detail you need to know how it is structured. You will find that Shakespeare's plays follow this general pattern.

1. **Introduction** of the characters.

2. **Problem(s) emerge** and/or confusion occurs – chain of events begins.

3. **Chaos follows** – one event leads to another.

4. **Climax of play** – in a tragedy this leads to the death of one or more characters, in a comedy confusions are sorted out.

5. **Order** is re-established.

Make notes on each scene to build up a clear picture of how the play develops and how the scenes link together.

For more help see GCSE Success Guide pages 48–57

Shakespeare's language

Identify the language type

Most of the play that you are studying will be written in **blank verse**, although parts of it may be in **rhymed verse** and parts of it may be in **prose**. When writing about Shakespeare's use of language, it is very important that you explain and analyse the **effects** created.

Blank verse

The rhythm pattern of blank verse closely resembles human speech.

Each line consists of **iambic pentameters**. An **iamb** is an unstressed syllable followed by a stressed one. There are five iambs in each line, so each line consists of **ten syllables**.

But soft, what light through yonder window breaks

This gives a **ti tum ti tum ti tum ti tum ti tum** rhythm pattern.

Rhymed verse

Sometimes Shakespeare uses a pattern of rhymed lines. The rhymes usually come in pairs and are called **rhyming couplets**.

Rhymed verse is used to:

● End scenes and emphasise the closing of the action

● Emphasise a particular kind of atmosphere or to indicate that something is different.

For example, the witches in *Macbeth* speak mainly in couplets.

When shall we three meet again?
In thunder, lightening, or in rain?

Prose

Shakespeare also uses prose or 'ordinary' language in some parts of his plays.
It can be used for:

- The lower characters
- For comic exchanges
- By characters of all ranks to create a particular effect
- Reading aloud of letters, proclamations, etc.

> Well, sir. My mistress is the sweetest lady – Lord, Lord! When 'twas a prating little thing! O, there is a nobleman in town, one Paris, that would fain lay knife aboard; but she, good soul, had as lief see a toad, a very toad, as see him.

REMEMBER

Look at what is happening at a particular point in the play to see **why** Shakespeare has chosen to use a particular kind of language.

Imagery

The use of imagery, often including **metaphors** and **similes**, is an important aspect of Shakespeare's language.

- It creates a vivid impression of the thing being described.

> So shows a snowy dove trooping with crows As yonder lady o'er her fellows shows.

- It creates a powerful emotional impact through the use of emotionally charged words and phrases.
- It adds emphasis to a particular idea.
- It emphasises a theme of the play through the repetition of certain images, e.g. the repeated use of 'heaven/hell' imagery to emphasise the conflict between good and evil in *Othello*.

> Divinity of hell! When devils will their blackest sins put on, They do suggest at first with heavenly shows,

For more help see GCSE Success Guide pages 48–57

Writing about themes

What are themes?

All of Shakespeare's plays are concerned with certain ideas or issues that recur and develop as the play progresses. These ideas or issues are the play's themes.

One of the reasons why Shakespeare's plays are still so popular today is that the themes they deal with are often universal issues which remain relevant to modern society.

Key themes in Shakespeare's plays

REMEMBER

Shakespeare does not explore all these themes in all the plays, but he does return to them again and again. Make sure that you know the key themes that Shakespeare explores in the play you are studying.

For more help see GCSE Success Guide pages 48–57

Writing about characters

Understanding Shakespeare's characters

As part of your study of a Shakespeare play, you will need to have a good understanding of how Shakespeare presents his characters and how they function in the play.

There are a number of ways in which you can gather information to build up a picture of how a character is presented:

- Descriptions of physical appearance – usually seen through the dialogue
- What the character says and how the character says it
- What the character thinks (often seen through asides and soliloquies)
- How the character acts and how their actions match their words
- What other characters say about a character
- How a character changes and develops during the course of the play.

Soliloquies and asides

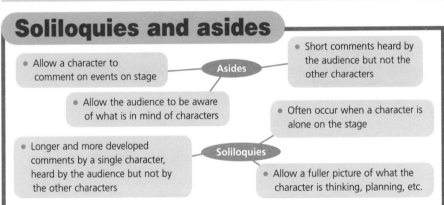

- Allow a character to comment on events on stage

Asides

- Short comments heard by the audience but not the other characters

- Allow the audience to be aware of what is in mind of characters

- Often occur when a character is alone on the stage

- Longer and more developed comments by a single character, heard by the audience but not by the other characters

Soliloquies

- Allow a fuller picture of what the character is thinking, planning, etc.

Be familiar with all the soliloquies of the characters you are studying and the **purpose** they perform.

REMEMBER

Characters in the play are not real people, so do not write about them as if they are. They are creations of Shakespeare. Be aware of the ways they are presented.

For more help see GCSE Success Guide pages 48–57

Planning and writing your Shakespeare assignment

Possible tasks

- An essay focusing on a particular character or characters' presentation and function
- A comparison of characters
- An examination of the themes
- An examination of the structure
- An analysis of a particular scene
- An analysis of an aspect of the language used, e.g. imagery
- A discussion of the dramatic effects used
- A discussion of a performance or comparison of performances.

Planning your Shakespeare assignment

1. Look carefully at the **question**. Make sure you understand what it involves and the best way of approaching it.

2. **Research** the task and gather your ideas.

3. Write a **plan** of how you are going to write the assignment.
   This should include the **structure → content → evidence** of your work.

4. Sort out your ideas into **paragraph** headings.

5. Link relevant **quotations** and textual references to the points you make.
   Use the **point → evidence → comment** approach.

6. Write the **first draft** of your assignment.

7. **Check** it through carefully.

8. Write your **final draft**.

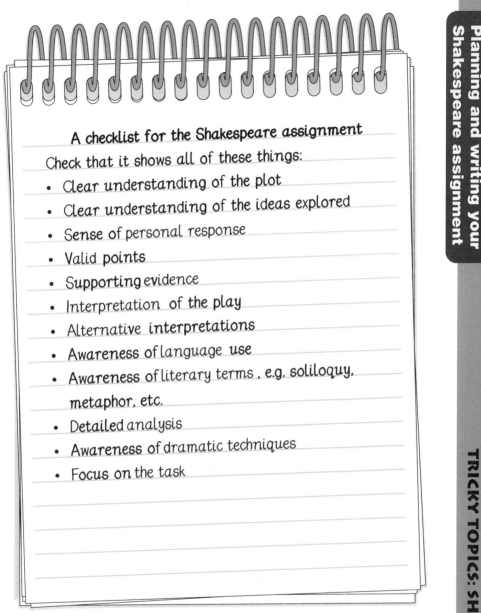

A checklist for the Shakespeare assignment

Check that it shows all of these things:

- Clear understanding of the plot
- Clear understanding of the ideas explored
- Sense of personal response
- Valid points
- Supporting evidence
- Interpretation of the play
- Alternative interpretations
- Awareness of language use
- Awareness of literary terms, e.g. soliloquy, metaphor, etc.
- Detailed analysis
- Awareness of dramatic techniques
- Focus on the task

REMEMBER

If your assignment is going to be used for GCSE English Literature, you will be required to show your awareness of historical, cultural and literary traditions.

For more help see GCSE Success Guide pages 48–57

Studying novels

Approaching the text

When studying a novel, the first thing you must do is read the text and get a clear impression of the **plot** or storyline.

Here is a method of approach.

1. Read the text through from beginning to end to get an overall understanding of the storyline.

2. Write a **summary** or a flow diagram outlining the key points of the **plot**.

3. Make a list of the **key characters**, where they appear and who they are.

4. Now go back and look over the story again and draw a plan of the **structure** of the story.

Gathering detail

As you study the novel in more detail you should keep notes on:

- The **narrative viewpoint** – who tells the story (i.e. first-person or third-person narration)
- The **characters** – who they are, what they do, how they relate to other characters, their function in the story
- The **setting** and **context** of the story – where it is set, when it is set
- The ways in which the writer uses **language** and the effects this creates
- The **style** of the writer.

Possible tasks

- An analysis of the presentation of a character/characters
- A discussion of the themes
- An examination of the writer's use of settings
- An examination of the writer's use of language
- An examination of the structure of the novel
- A close analysis of a chapter or episode

A novel assignment checklist

- Focus on the topic or question.
- Think about the narrative viewpoint and the effect it has on the play.
- Demonstrate sound knowledge of the text.
- Show awareness of the structure of the novel.
- Show awareness of the themes explored.
- Understand the ways in which the writer presents characters.
- Understand the ways in which language is used.
- Analyse the effects created through the use of language.
- Be aware of the setting of the story.
- Understand the context.

REMEMBER

If you are entering for GCSE English Literature your assignment should show an awareness of the social, historical or cultural context of the novel.

For more help see GCSE Success Guide pages 78–82

Looking at character

How authors create character

Characters are central to a novel and you need to be clear about who they are and how the writer presents them.

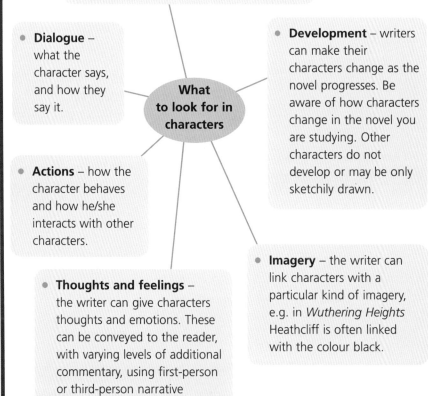

- **Physical description** – what the character looks like, how he/she dresses, etc. The character's name may also tell you something about their personality or function, e.g. Mr Knightley in *Emma*.

- **Dialogue** – what the character says, and how they say it.

- **Actions** – how the character behaves and how he/she interacts with other characters.

What to look for in characters

- **Development** – writers can make their characters change as the novel progresses. Be aware of how characters change in the novel you are studying. Other characters do not develop or may be only sketchily drawn.

- **Imagery** – the writer can link characters with a particular kind of imagery, e.g. in *Wuthering Heights* Heathcliff is often linked with the colour black.

- **Thoughts and feelings** – the writer can give characters thoughts and emotions. These can be conveyed to the reader, with varying levels of additional commentary, using first-person or third-person narrative techniques.

Dialogue

The speech between characters can form an important element in the story.

- Helps the reader to form an impression of the character

- Makes characters seem more vivid and lifelike

- Reveals things about the character's personality, motives and beliefs

- Shows what characters think about other characters

- Relates to broader themes and ideas expressed in the novel

Checklist of things to look for when examining characters

- Their actions
- What they say
- What others say about them
- How they interact with others
- How they change and develop
- The language used to present them

REMEMBER

Characters are not real people, they are the creations of the writer. Be aware of how the writer uses language to present the characters.

For more help see GCSE Success Guide pages 78–82

Exploring themes, mood and atmosphere

Themes

Novels and short stories, as well as simply 'telling a story', often explore themes. A **theme** is an idea that lies behind the story. Novels and short stories can often be concerned with more than one theme.

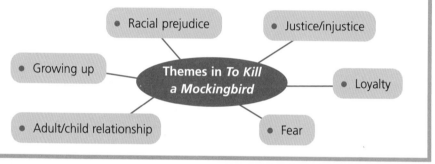

- Racial prejudice
- Justice/injustice
- Growing up
- Themes in *To Kill a Mockingbird*
- Loyalty
- Adult/child relationship
- Fear

Mood and atmosphere

Writers create a sense of **mood** and **atmosphere** in their stories. Often the mood and atmosphere of a story are closely linked to its setting and its characters.

Writers use various techniques to establish a sense of mood and atmosphere:

- Effective use of description
- Careful choice of vocabulary
- Variation of sentence length, e.g. short sentences can suggest tension or action, longer ones can slow the pace or create a more tranquil mood
- Repetition of words or phrases
- Use of monologue (a character speaking to him or herself)
- Use of literary techniques, such as:
  - metaphors
  - personification
  - oxymorons
  - alliteration
  - assonance
- Use of motifs (words, ideas and images which recur in texts)
- Use of the senses: sound, touch, sight, smell, taste
- Careful use of the tone of the narrator.

A checklist on studying themes, mood and atmosphere

- Think carefully about the themes explored.
- Identify the ideas that the writer is putting forward.
- Make notes on each of the themes.
- Include page references in your notes – these will help you to refer back to particular sections.
- Look at the kind of language the writer uses to present and explore themes.
- Use brief quotations where appropriate.
- Understand **how** the writer creates a sense of place or setting.
- Look at the use of description.
- Be aware of the mood and atmosphere created.
- Examine the **effects** of the use of particular literary techniques.

REMEMBER

Focus on the ways in which writers use language to create atmosphere and tone and explore themes.

For more help see GCSE Success Guide pages 78–82

Short stories

Short story structure

Many of the features that are found in novels are also found in short stories. But short stories are different in some ways too.

- Obviously a short story is much shorter than a novel. Sometimes this is because the material the writer has chosen to write about is quite narrow. Sometimes the material is broad but the writer has chosen to focus on just one aspect of it to maximise the story's impact.

- Short stories usually contain fewer characters because there simply isn't enough space to develop a lot of characters in any depth.

- Many short stories focus on a single incident, moment in time or experience. This is often a point of climax or a crisis point. Alternatively, the experience can be a 'snap-shot' of ordinary life.

- Short stories often pay less attention to setting and background information and focus instead on characters, action or dialogue.

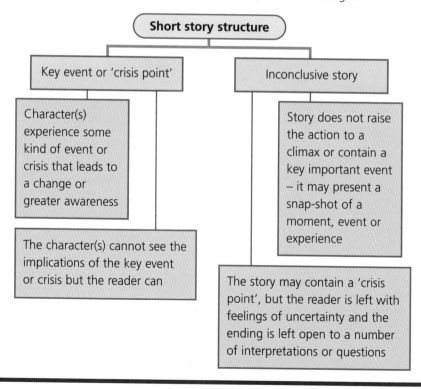

Short story structure

Key event or 'crisis point'

Character(s) experience some kind of event or crisis that leads to a change or greater awareness

The character(s) cannot see the implications of the key event or crisis but the reader can

Inconclusive story

Story does not raise the action to a climax or contain a key important event – it may present a snap-shot of a moment, event or experience

The story may contain a 'crisis point', but the reader is left with feelings of uncertainty and the ending is left open to a number of interpretations or questions

Beginnings

Beginnings and endings are obviously very important parts of a short story.

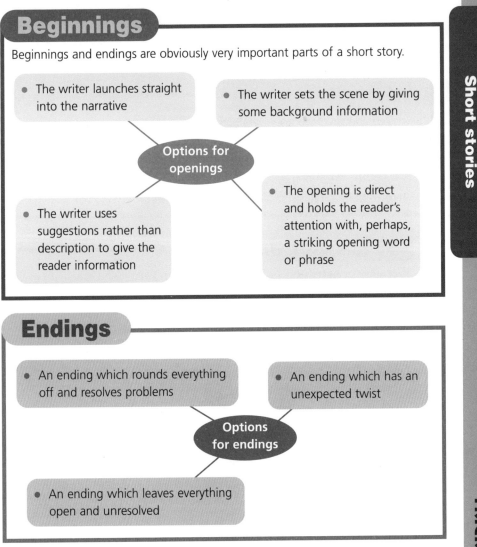

- The writer launches straight into the narrative

- The writer sets the scene by giving some background information

Options for openings

- The writer uses suggestions rather than description to give the reader information

- The opening is direct and holds the reader's attention with, perhaps, a striking opening word or phrase

Endings

- An ending which rounds everything off and resolves problems

- An ending which has an unexpected twist

Options for endings

- An ending which leaves everything open and unresolved

REMEMBER

All the techniques that writers use when writing novels can be used in short story writing.

For more help see GCSE Success Guide pages 83–85

The narrator

Types of narration

Both novels and short stories have a narrator from whose viewpoint the story is told. One of the first things to establish when studying your text is the type of **narrative viewpoint**. There are two basic types of narration:

- First-person narration
- Third-person narration.

First-person narration

In a **first-person narrative** the story is told by a character who is actually in the story. The 'I' narrator tells of the events that he or she experiences. This kind of narration can be found in many novels and short stories, such as Charlotte Bronte's *Jane Eyre* or Charles Dickens' *Great Expectations*.

> Squire Trelawney, Dr Livesey, and the rest of these gentlemen having asked me to write down the whole particulars about Treasure Island, from the beginning to the end, keeping nothing back but the bearings of the island, and that only because there is still treasure not yet lifted, I take up my pen...

(from *Treasure Island* by Robert Louis Stevenson)

- Allows the reader to 'see' directly into the mind of the narrator.

Features of first-person narration

- As this form of narration only gives us the narrator's view, it can present a biased view of events.

- Sometimes the events can be told from the present time, looking back on the past, so the narrator's view can change as time goes by.

For more help see GCSE Success Guide pages 78–85

Third-person narration

In a third-person narrative, the narrator sees and knows everything that is going on (also called the omniscient narrator). The story is told directly to the reader by the narrator.

The narrator in this kind of text can be either intrusive or unintrusive.

● The **intrusive narrator** enters into the novel or story by making comments on the events or characters. Thomas Hardy and Jane Austen, for example, do this a lot in their novels.

> Every reader of a sentimental turn (and we desire no other) must have been pleased with the *tableau* with which the last act of our little drama concluded…

(from *Vanity Fair* by William Makepeace Thackeray)

● The **unintrusive narrator** tells the story from a distance and does not make judgements or voice opinions on the characters or what is happening.

Features of third-person narration

- Allows the narrator to know what is going on in the minds of the characters.
- Allows the narrator to move from one scene to another.
- Allows the narrator to be distanced from the characters.

Other types of narration

Two other kinds of narrative techniques that you might see are:

● **Internal monologue** – a single character gives their thoughts and feelings, as in Alan Bennett's *Talking Heads*

● **Stream of consciousness** – thoughts are written down randomly as if straight from the character's mind in an unstructured and unpunctuated way, as used by James Joyce and Virginia Woolf.

REMEMBER

Whatever technique the writer uses, they have chosen it specifically in order to create the **effects** that they want.

Personal writing: fiction

Imaginative writing

As part of your assessment for GCSE English, you will need to write to 'explore, imagine and entertain'. This will usually involve producing a piece of personal, imaginative writing.

Possible assignments

- The opening to a short story
- A whole short story of your own
- Fictional descriptions of people and places which aim to entertain, interest or amuse the reader
- A selection of your own poetry
- A diary kept by an imaginary character
- A piece of fictional dialogue between imaginary characters
- A section of playscript.

Planning your narrative

1. Write down all your **initial ideas** on paper.

2. Plan the outline of your story. A good, gripping **plot** is essential.

3. Decide on your main **characters** and perhaps two or three other characters. (Your story will be quite short so don't try to include too many characters.) Your characters need to be interesting and convincing – see the checklist on the next page!

4. Decide on how you will present the **setting** of your story.

5. Structure your ideas so that you know how your story will develop.

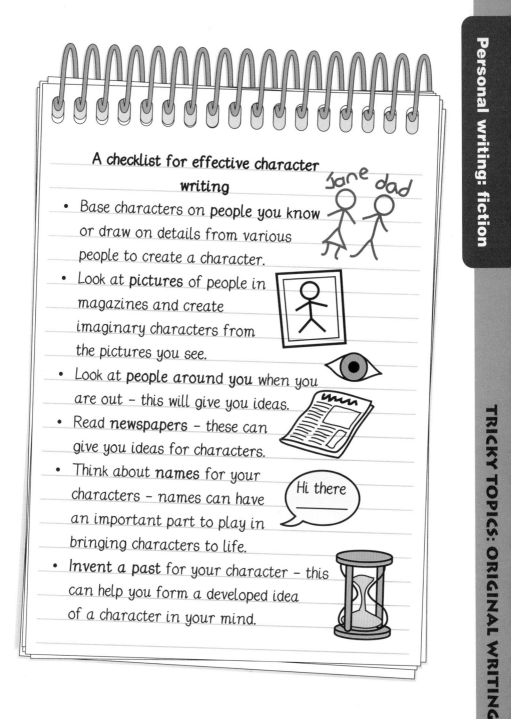

A checklist for effective character writing

- Base characters on **people you know** or draw on details from various people to create a character.
- Look at **pictures** of people in magazines and create imaginary characters from the pictures you see.
- Look at **people around you** when you are out – this will give you ideas.
- Read **newspapers** – these can give you ideas for characters.
- Think about **names** for your characters – names can have an important part to play in bringing characters to life.
- Invent a **past** for your character – this can help you form a developed idea of a character in your mind.

Personal writing: non-fiction

Factual writing

As part of your course, you will need to complete a piece of non-fiction writing, i.e. based on actual events or factual material. This may be produced as a coursework assignment, or you might write about this in the exam.

The purpose of this kind of writing is to 'inform, explain and describe'. Whatever the topic of your writing, you need to be fully aware of the **audience** and **purpose** of your piece.

Possible tasks

- An autobiographical piece – you could describe a particular episode or event you have experienced
- A biographical piece based on the life of someone who interests you
- A piece of continuous writing which describes your feelings on a particular topic or situation
- A piece of continuous writing which describes your point of view on a particular subject
- An article for a magazine
- A discursive essay explaining two sides of an issue
- An account of an actual event
- Entries in a reference book or encyclopaedia
- Advice leaflets
- Newspaper articles

Language use

You should:

- Use clear and straightforward language
- Structure your ideas logically
- Keep to the point.

Planning your non-fiction writing

- Decide on your **topic**.

- Decide on the **form** your writing will take – bearing in mind audience and purpose.

- **Research** your ideas if you need to. For example, if you are writing a biographical piece you may need to check details.

- **Make notes** on your material. Spidergrams can be useful in making your notes.

- **Use your notes** to plan your ideas.

- Plan the **structure** of your writing.

- Write a **first draft** of your work.

- **Check** this through carefully for spelling, punctuation and expression.

- Produce your **final draft** after making any corrections/alterations required.

A checklist for effective non-fiction writing

- Organise your work effectively.
- Research your topic carefully.
- Write in continuous prose.
- Make your writing interesting.
- Use descriptive techniques.
- Show effective use of language.
- Write accurately.
- Make sure that your writing is in your own words.

For more help see GCSE Success Guide pages 34–35

Preparing and presenting your coursework

What is the written coursework worth?

Written coursework will form 20% of the total marks for your GCSE English course and 30% of the total marks for GCSE English Literature. It is important to make sure that you prepare your coursework carefully and that you present it as effectively as you can.

Preparing the coursework

1. Always **plan** your assignments carefully. As part of your planning, **structure** your work effectively, e.g. organise the different elements into paragraphs and choose an order for them.

2. Always do a **first draft** so that you can cross out and change things around as you are working.

3. If your first draft contains a lot of changes and alterations, it is advisable to **re-draft** this.

4. Your **teacher** is allowed to look at your draft and to give general advice. You can then decide what alterations you might want to make before producing the final draft. Your teacher is not allowed to mark your work at this stage, or correct errors or proof-read it for you.

5. Write your **final draft** of the work.

6. **Proof-read** your final draft, making sure that you correct any spelling, punctuation or phrasing errors. (If you find any major mistakes, you can always re-draft it again if you need to.)

7. When you are completely happy with it, hand it in to your teacher for **marking**.

Note: Once your teacher has marked it, you are not allowed to re-draft it again.

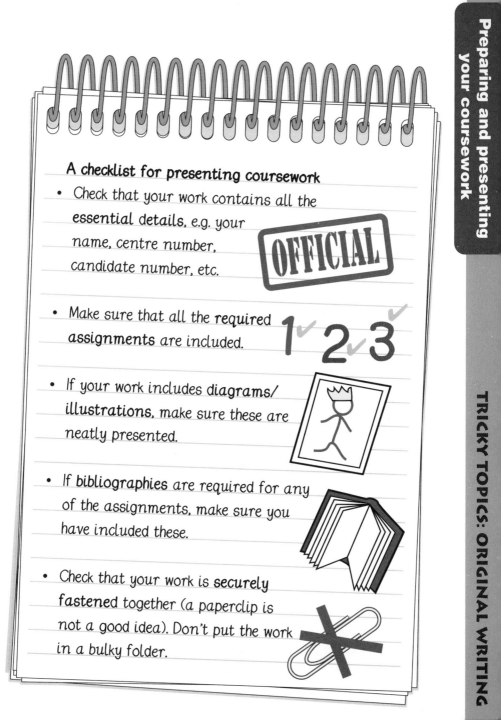

A checklist for presenting coursework

- Check that your work contains all the essential details, e.g. your name, centre number, candidate number, etc.

- Make sure that all the required assignments are included.

- If your work includes diagrams/ illustrations, make sure these are neatly presented.

- If bibliographies are required for any of the assignments, make sure you have included these.

- Check that your work is securely fastened together (a paperclip is not a good idea). Don't put the work in a bulky folder.

Understanding Speaking and Listening

What is the oral coursework worth?

Your oral coursework mark will form 20% of your total mark for GCSE English.

In this element of the course, you will be assessed in three key contexts:

1. An extended individual contribution

2. A drama-focused activity

3. Discussion work in pairs or larger groups.

Your best mark in each of the three key contexts will be used for your assignment. These three areas might involve you in a range of activities.

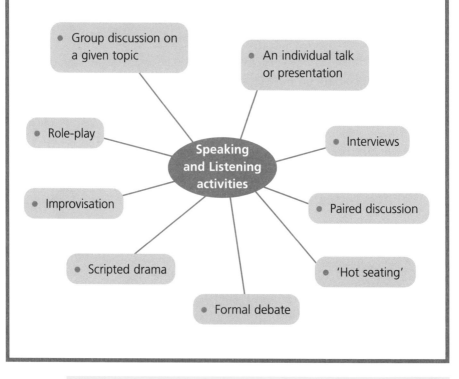

- Group discussion on a given topic
- An individual talk or presentation
- Role-play
- Interviews
- Improvisation
- Paired discussion
- Scripted drama
- 'Hot seating'
- Formal debate

Speaking and Listening activities

For more help see **GCSE Success Guide** pages **24–25**

Where and when?

- It is likely that most if not all of your oral assessments will take place in a classroom context. However, your teacher might use an area such as the school hall or drama studio for some of the activities.

- Your teacher might set up a specific activity for your Speaking and Listening assessment. If this is the case, you will probably be told beforehand that an assessment is going to take place.

- Your teacher can also make assessments on a more informal basis, such as contributions made to class and groups discussions.

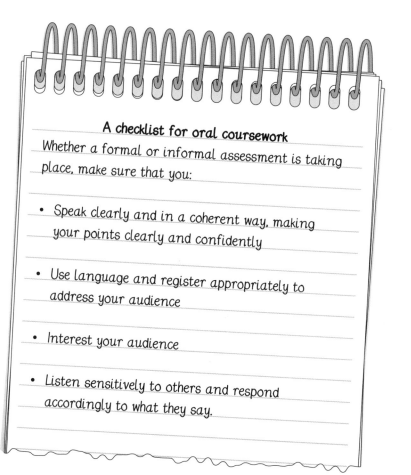

A checklist for oral coursework

Whether a formal or informal assessment is taking place, make sure that you:

- Speak clearly and in a coherent way, making your points clearly and confidently

- Use language and register appropriately to address your audience

- Interest your audience

- Listen sensitively to others and respond accordingly to what they say.

Preparing an individual talk

What is an individual talk?

It is likely that the extended individual contribution will take the form of a prepared talk of some kind. You might give this talk to your teacher, or a group of students, or the whole class.

You will need to be clear whether you are giving an **informal talk** or a **formal talk** because each has its own individual style and features. Your teacher should tell you which you are meant to do.

- You might sit down to give the talk
- Allow the audience to interrupt with questions as you go along
- You will not be allowed notes
- Use a relaxed and informal tone and approach

In an informal talk …

- You might be allowed notes
- You would usually stand
- Questions should come at the end, not during the talk
- You might be further away from your audience and so need to project your voice more
- Your tone and attitude should be more formal

In a formal talk …

REMEMBER

Whatever kind of talk you are giving, make sure that you are aware of the **purpose** of your talk and that you address it to suit your **audience**.

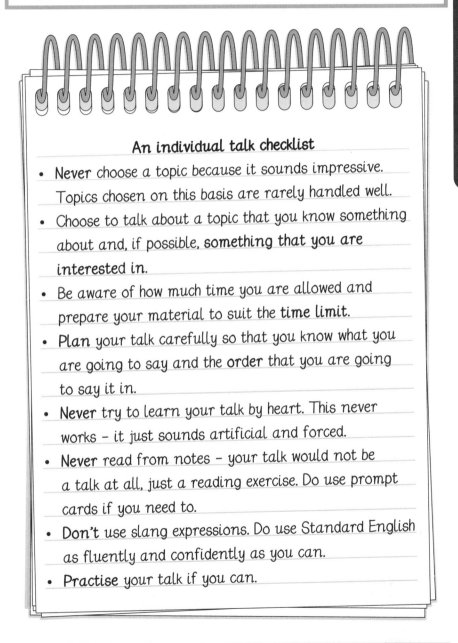

An individual talk checklist

- **Never** choose a topic because it sounds impressive. Topics chosen on this basis are rarely handled well.
- Choose to talk about a topic that you know something about and, if possible, **something that you are interested in.**
- Be aware of how much time you are allowed and prepare your material to suit the **time limit.**
- **Plan** your talk carefully so that you know what you are going to say and the **order** that you are going to say it in.
- **Never** try to learn your talk by heart. This never works – it just sounds artificial and forced.
- **Never** read from notes – your talk would not be a talk at all, just a reading exercise. Do use prompt cards if you need to.
- **Don't** use slang expressions. Do use Standard English as fluently and confidently as you can.
- **Practise** your talk if you can.

For more help see **GCSE Success Guide** pages **24–29**

What is a group discussion?

Group discussion is an element in the assessment of Speaking and Listening. The group might be a small group within the class or it might be the whole class. It is most likely that you will be asked to take part in an **informal discussion**. Your teacher might also hold a **formal debate** at some point in your course.

Planning a group discussion

- In a formal discussion, a chairperson might be given the task of chairing the discussion and preventing people from being interrupted.

- If you need a record of the views, decisions, etc. discussed in your group, make sure that you agree who is to take the notes before the discussion starts.

- Try to make sure that your chairs are positioned in a way that will help you to talk to others. Sitting in a line behind desks is not a good way to try to discuss with others. Move your chairs to form a circle, or group around a desk.

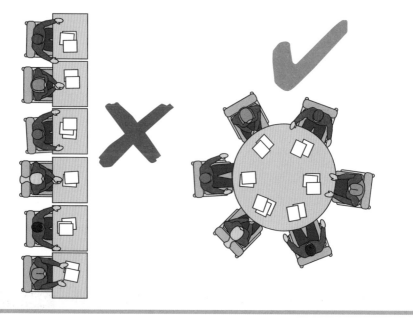

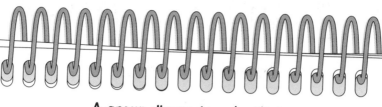

A group discussion checklist

- **Listen** to other people's views. Remember, this is Speaking and Listening. Listening is as important as speaking.
- **Don't** try to dominate the discussion – make a point then let someone else have a chance.
- **Say what you feel.** Don't feel that you can only agree with other people.
- **Try to see other people's views**, even though you might not agree with them.
- **Keep involved** and respond to what other people have to say. Don't switch off.
- **Support** other people's points if you agree with them.
- **Involve others.** Try to bring into the discussion those who have not said much.
- **Don't** bolt in when someone else is speaking.
- Avoid slang and swearing and speak clearly using Standard English.
- If the teacher or an examiner is sitting with you, don't talk just to them – **talk to the group**.

TRICKY TOPICS: SPEAKING AND LISTENING COURSEWORK

Drama activities

What is a drama activity?

As part of your assessment for Speaking and Listening, you will need to take part in some kind of drama-based activity. This kind of activity can take various forms.

Acting out a scene from a play with other students

Rehearsed speeches – individuals prepare a speech from a play and recite it to the group

Miming a scene using only body and facial expressions

Improvising scenes from a play

Recording key scenes, either on tape or video, and analysing effects/performance as a group

Drama is ...

Making director's notes on a scene and presenting them with an explanatory commentary to the group

Putting a character on trial, with group members appointed as prosecution, defence and jury

Two groups play a scene in different ways and then discuss different interpretations

Groups plan staging/movement of a particular scene

Media reports and interviews on characters

Improvising an 'extra' scene either from before the play starts or after it has ended

'Hotseating' – one person takes the role of a character and is asked questions by others in the group about why he/she has done what they have done, etc.

'Split personalities' – two students are allocated a character, one student speaks the words, then the other says what the character might be thinking at that point in the play

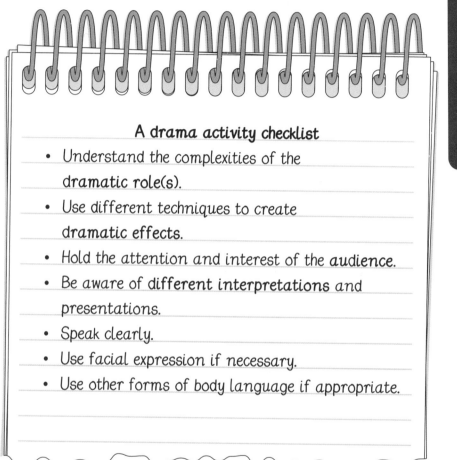

A drama activity checklist

- Understand the complexities of the dramatic role(s).
- Use different techniques to create dramatic effects.
- Hold the attention and interest of the audience.
- Be aware of different interpretations and presentations.
- Speak clearly.
- Use facial expression if necessary.
- Use other forms of body language if appropriate.

REMEMBER

This kind of activity is used as part of your assessment on Speaking and Listening. You should speak in Standard English unless the role requires a different form of English.

For more help see **GCSE Success Guide** pages **24–27**

Effective Speaking and Listening

What is the examiner looking for?

Your teacher/examiner will expect to see that you can do the following things:

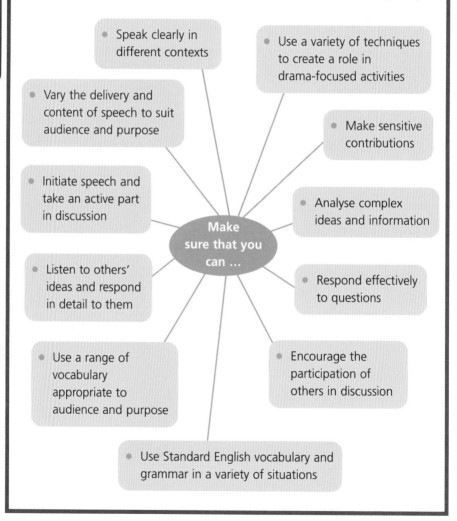

- Speak clearly in different contexts
- Use a variety of techniques to create a role in drama-focused activities
- Vary the delivery and content of speech to suit audience and purpose
- Make sensitive contributions
- Initiate speech and take an active part in discussion
- Analyse complex ideas and information
- Listen to others' ideas and respond in detail to them
- Respond effectively to questions
- Use a range of vocabulary appropriate to audience and purpose
- Encourage the participation of others in discussion
- Use Standard English vocabulary and grammar in a variety of situations

Make sure that you can ...

A checklist for improving Speaking and Listening work

- Join in class discussions whenever they happen, not just ones that you know are going to be formally assessed. Get used to contributing to discussion.
- Ask questions in class. This can sometimes prompt discussion with the teacher and other students.
- Answer questions in class (don't be the one that tries to monopolise things, though, by answering every question).
- In paired or group discussions, listen carefully to others and respond constructively to this. In paired discussions, the discussion should be fairly evenly balanced and so there needs to be co-operation between you and your partner.
- Know the rules and procedures for formal debates – your teacher will explain these to you beforehand.
- When you give an individual talk, make sure that you prepare enough material.

For more help see GCSE Success Guide pages 24–29

Glossary

alliteration the repetition of the same consonant sound, especially at the beginning of several consecutive words in the same line, e.g. 'Five miles meandering in a mazy motion'

aside words spoken by a character on stage that are not intended to be heard by the other characters present

assonance the repetition of similar vowel sounds, e.g. 'Summer grows old, cold-blooded mother'

atmosphere the pervading feeling created by a description of the setting or the action, e.g. foreboding, happiness

audience the people addressed by a piece of writing, speech, etc.; associated with the idea of purpose

aural imagery images created through sound by the use of techniques such as alliteration, assonance and onomatopoeia

autobiography an account of a person's life written by him or herself

ballad traditionally, a song telling a story; often used to describe a narrative poem

bias language used in such a way as to give a prejudiced view against someone or something or which favours a particular point of view

biography a written account or history of the life of an individual written by someone else

blank verse unrhymed poetry that adheres to a strict pattern in that each line is an iambic pentameter (a ten-syllable line with five stresses); close to the rhythm of speech or prose

caesura a conscious break in a line of poetry

characterisation the variety of techniques that writers use to create and present their characters, including description of their appearance, their actions, their speech and how other characters react to them

climax the most important event in the story or play

complication the main action of the play, in which the characters respond to the dramatic incitement and other developments that arise from it

conjunction a word which joins clauses together, e.g. and, but

connotation an association attached to a word or phrase in addition to its dictionary definition

context the circumstance in which speech or writing takes place

contraction a shortened word, e.g. isn't, don't

couplet two lines of verse which rhyme

crisis the climax of a play or story

denouement near the ending of a play, novel or drama, where the plot is resolved

dialogue speech between two or more people

direct speech the words that are actually spoken

drama a composition intended for performance before an audience

dramatic incitement the incident which provides the starting point for the main action of the play

dramatic irony a situation in a play, the irony of which is clear to the audience but not to the characters, e.g. in *Twelfth Night*, where Olivia and Orsino do not know that 'Caesario' (Viola) is really a girl disguised as a boy

enjambment a line of verse that flows on to the next line without a break

episode a scene within a narrative that develops or is connected to the main story

episodic containing different stories or narratives linked together

exposition the opening of the play which introduces characters and sets the scene

fact something which has been established as true and correct

fiction a story that is invented, i.e. it is not factual, though it may be based on events that actually happened

figurative language language that is symbolic or metaphorical and not meant to be taken literally

form the way a poem is structured or laid out

free verse a form of poetry not using obvious rhyme patterns or a consistent metre

hyperbole deliberate and extravagant exaggeration

iambic pentameter a line of verse containing five feet, each foot having an unstressed syllable followed by a stressed syllable

imagery the use of words to create a picture or image in the reader's mind

imperatives commands

indirect speech words of a speaker that are reported rather than being quoted directly

interior monologue similar to a soliloquy, a character talking to him or herself, e.g. in Bennett's *Talking Heads*

interview a meeting between two people, e.g. a journalist and a celebrity, using questioning and discussion to ascertain information or for entertainment value

irony the conveyance of a meaning that is opposite to the literal meaning of the words, e.g. 'This is a fine time to tell me' (when it is actually an inappropriate time); a situation or outcome which has a significance unforeseen at the time

language of advertising features and techniques commonly found in advertising, e.g. appealing adjectives, exaggeration

metaphor figure of speech in which a person or thing is described as *being* the thing it resembles, e.g. 'she's a tiger' to describe a ferocious person

mood the atmosphere created by a piece of writing

narrative a piece of writing that tells a story

narration, first-person the telling of a story through the voice of a character in their own words, e.g. 'I went to the fair, even though I hated it'

narration, third-person the telling of a story through the voice of the author describing the actions of the characters, e.g. 'He went to the fair, even though he hated it'

narrative structure the way that a piece of story-writing has been put together, e.g. in a novel, the development of the plot through the arrangement of chapters and who is telling the story

narrative techniques the ways in which an author tells a story

narrator the person telling the story

objective information factual details

onomatopoeia when a word sounds like the noise it describes, e.g. 'pop' or 'the murmuring of innumerable bees'

opinion a view held by some but not necessarily by others

oxymoron a figure of speech that places words of opposite meanings together, e.g. bitter sweet

personification the attribution of human feelings, emotions or sensations to an inanimate object; a kind of metaphor where human qualities are given to things or abstract ideas

plot the main story or scheme of connected events running through a play or novel

poetic voice the 'speaker' of the poem; the 'voice' of the poem might be that of the poet but it could be that of a character or persona from the poet's imagination

preview a kind of report on a film, programme, book, etc. that is soon to be released

prose any kind of writing which is not verse, usually divided into fiction and non-fiction

purpose the reason for the communication

regular metre a regular succession of groups of long and short, stressed and unstressed syllables in which poetry is often written

resolution the final section of a play or story, where the action is resolved and a conclusion is reached

review usually a kind of report on a film, programme, book, etc. that has already been released

rhetorical question question raised in speech that does not require an answer (used for effect)

rhyme corresponding sounds in words, often at the end of a poetic line (can also occur within lines)

rhyming couplet two rhyming lines of verse

rhythm the 'movement' of a poem, as created by the metre and the way that language is stressed within the poem

setting the period of time and the place in which a story is set

simile figure of speech in which a person or thing is described as being *like* another, usually preceded by 'as' or 'like', e.g. 'she's like a tiger' to describe a ferocious person

snapshots separate descriptions of the stages in a sequence

soliloquy a speech in which a character in a play expresses their thoughts and feelings aloud for the benefit of the audience, but not for the other characters, often in a revealing way

sonnet a fourteen-line poem, usually with ten syllables in each line – there are several ways in which the lines can be organised, but often they consist of an octave and sestet

stanza the blocks of lines into which a poem is divided, forming a definite pattern

stream of consciousness a narrative form where random thoughts give the impression that the words have spilled straight from the narrator's mind

structure the way that a piece of story-writing has been put together, e.g. in a novel, the development of the plot through the arrangement of chapters

style the particular way in which writers use language to express their ideas

subjective information personal opinions and feelings

sub-plot a less important part of a story, that is connected to and develops the main plot

symbolism similar to imagery; symbols are things that represent something else, e.g. red roses are given to loved ones because they symbolise love

textual analysis a detailed consideration of the features of a text, to build a view of how the text achieves its various effects

theme a central idea that the writer explores through a text, e.g. love, loss, revenge

tone created through the combined effects of the author's rhythm and diction

voice the speaker of the poem or prose, either the poet or author's own voice or that of an invented character

Every effort has been made to contact the holders of copyright material, but if any have been inadvertently overlooked the publishers will be pleased to make the necessary arrangements at the first opportunity.

Letts Educational
4 Grosvenor Place
London SW1X 7DL
School enquiries: 01539 564910
Parent & student enquiries: 01539 564913
E-mail: mail@lettsed.co.uk
Website: www.letts-educational.com

Text © Steven Croft 2005.
Design and illustration © Letts Educational Ltd 2005.

First published 2005

10 9 8 7 6 5 4 3

ISBN 9781843154693

The author asserts his moral right to be identified as the author of this work.

British Library Cataloguing in Publication Data

A catalogue record for this book is available from the British Library.

Acknowledgements

Cover design by Big Top.

Commissioned by Cassie Birmingham

Project management for Letts by Julia Swales

Edited by Vicky Butt

Design and project management by Ken Vail Graphic Design, Cambridge

Printed in Dubai